"The paranormal is now back in f[...] has given us a well-documented e[...] backgrounds, teachings and errors of well-known figures in this field. *The Paranormal Conspiracy* is a powerful refutation of this whole dangerous movement."

Walter A. Elwell, Ph.D., professor emeritus of biblical and theological studies, Wheaton College, Wheaton, Illinois

"With biblical perspective, Dr. Dailey has assessed satanic control through lies and deceptions over mankind. His research produces intriguing narratives and exposure of popular persons, groups, behaviors and religions. Good research and evaluation of demonic influences in current society. You will be surprised. Well written and well worth reading!"

C. Fred Dickason, Th.D., professor emeritus and former chair of theology, Moody Bible Institute, Chicago, Illinois

"Tim Dailey has taken on a difficult but very important subject, and he has succeeded! Read the book, folks. Read the book."

Jim Valentine, director, Christian Apologetics: Research and Information Service

"*MythBusters* meets *This Present Darkness* in Tim Dailey's gripping new book, *The Paranormal Conspiracy*. With compelling narratives backed by his usual meticulous research, Dailey warns that those involved in the occult are neither finding enlightenment nor playing with a fantasy—but rather, are courting danger for themselves and their families."

Peter Sprigg, senior fellow for policy studies, Family Research Council, Washington, D.C.

THE
PARANORMAL
CONSPIRACY

THE TRUTH ABOUT GHOSTS, ALIENS
AND MYSTERIOUS BEINGS

TIMOTHY DAILEY, Ph.D.

Chosen

a division of Baker Publishing Group
Minneapolis, Minnesota

Published by Chosen Books
11400 Hampshire Avenue South
Bloomington, Minnesota 55438
www.chosenbooks.com

Chosen Books is a division of
Baker Publishing Group, Grand Rapids, Michigan

Printed in the United States of America

Library of Congress Cataloging-in-Publication Data
Dailey, Timothy J.
The paranormal conspiracy : the truth about ghosts, aliens and mysterious beings / Timothy Dailey.
    pages cm
    Includes bibliographical references and index.
    Summary: "This biblically based, eye-opening book will help you understand the danger of the paranormal phenomenon by exposing the demonic agenda behind it"— Provided by publisher.
    ISBN 978-0-8007-9776-8 (pbk. : alk. paper)
    1. Parapsychology—Religious aspects—Christianity. 2. Occultism—Religious aspects—Christianity. I. Title.
    BR115.P85D35 2015
    261.5′13—dc23   2015005498

Cover design by Gearbox

15 16 17 18 19 20 21   7 6 5 4 3 2 1

It looked as if a night of dark intent
Was coming, and not only a night, an age.

—Robert Frost

For Rebekka

CONTENTS

1. Doctrines of Demons   9
2. The Doors of Perception   19
3. Beings of High Strangeness   30
4. Messengers of Deception   47
5. Unearthly Encounters   64
6. The Lost City of Z   83
7. The Great Scheme   97
8. Spirit Love   116
9. Theater of the Gods   130
10. The Mystery of Cicada 3301   145
11. The Zombie Apocalypse   162
12. The Restless Heart   177

Notes   193
Index   205

1

DOCTRINES OF DEMONS

Love is the ultimate and the highest goal to which man can aspire.

—Viktor Frankl

The photo went viral, like a dagger to the heart, an exquisite, ineffable wound penetrating to the deepest recesses of the soul. An elderly man sits alone at a table in a burger joint, minding his own business. And then we see what his business is: Carefully propped up on the table next to him is a framed photograph of the woman who shared his life for 55 years. The headline says it all: "Widower Keeps Late Wife's Memory Alive by Dining with Her Photo"—a simple, touching scene that speaks more than learned tomes about that which makes the world go 'round.

Madina Bashizadah, who posted the photo of the poignant scene on Twitter, later told the *Huffington Post*: "Automatically, I assumed she wasn't here with us and I started tearing up because it was such a beautiful moment, but heartbreaking at the same time." Eighty-seven-year-old John Silva was taken aback to learn that the photo had exploded across the Internet and become an international news item. It was the kind of fairy tale seldom witnessed in an age when, as it is written, "the love of many shall grow cold."

John's romance began on a dusty baseball field in New Bedford, Massachusetts, on his seventeenth birthday. It was September 1944, and his church team was battling for the league championship. John dropped the ball—literally—and went scrambling after it. Providentially, it rolled to the feet of a young lady, who playfully picked it up. Suddenly the ball game was the last thing on John's mind: "It was right there and then I fell in love with her. I told her within ten minutes I was going to marry her; it really was love at first sight."

But marriage was not to be—at least not then. When the game ended John looked for the object of his affections, but she had vanished. Then he spotted her amidst the crowd leaving the ballpark. Their eyes met and she blew him a kiss. John raced in her direction but lost sight of her. He did not even know her name.

Years passed. John began playing minor league baseball and scanned the crowds unfailingly for a glimpse of that bright smiling face. He was considered a very eligible bachelor, but had little interest in dating: "In my heart this was the woman I wanted to marry but I had no idea who she was. When people would ask me if I had a girlfriend tears would come to my eyes because I did, I just didn't know where to find her again."

Then, one day as John was delivering a load of potatoes to a customer's house, the door opened, and there like a dream she was, a glow of recognition on her face. Ten years had gone by, but Hilda had not forgotten him either. "Are you married?" popped out of John's mouth. She said no. "Have you got a boyfriend?" The answer was no again.

John was instantly down on one knee.

Theirs was a marriage "made in heaven" consisting of two people who each put the other first. Hilda gave up her career to move with John to California, and John retired from baseball to spend more time with his wife.

But nothing lasts forever—in this world anyway—and the unimaginable happened. In her later years Hilda slipped and fell, seriously injuring herself. After a stroke and a bout with cancer that left her unable to care for herself, John was forced to do what he vowed never to do: put his dear wife into a nursing home. For the next two and a half years he virtually lived at the facility, caring for her needs and spending his nights by her side. And then the heartsick ending came:

> It was a miracle. She opened her eyes and pushed herself forward with all of the strength she had left and said: "John, I love you. I've always loved you and in a million years you'll still be my husband."
>
> And then she put her head back and that was it. I put my head on her head.[1]

John's family closed ranks around him, worried that, overwhelmed by grief, he might try to end his own life. But

John says that is something he would never consider, and he would not do anything to jeopardize his anticipated happy reunion: "I am now just waiting for the day Hilda comes to get me so we can be together in Heaven forever."[2]

Man's Search for Meaning

John's story unleashed a torrent of online comments. One remark encapsulates the sentiments: "Don't we all wish someone loved us like that? . . . beautiful . . . and sad."[3] We can all recognize the universal aspiration for ultimate meaning that is somehow wrapped up in that ineffable, bewitching quantity called *love*.

Few have spoken with more authority regarding humankind's quest for meaning than Viktor Frankl, the renowned Austrian psychiatrist and holocaust survivor. Frankl's life collapsed as the Nazi regime descended upon Europe, sweeping away tens of millions in its violent wake. He and his new wife, Tilly, were deported to concentration camps and soon separated. Frankl endured unimaginable suffering.

One night, while on a forced march across frozen landscape with only thin garments to protect him from the icy wind, he overheard one of the prisoners: "If our wives could see us now! I do hope they are better off in their camps and don't know what is happening to us."[4]

It was then that Frankl realized that each of the men was thinking about his wife. He himself had a luminous vision of Tilly, smiling at him from above:

A thought transfixed me: for the first time in my life I saw the truth as it is set into song by so many poets, proclaimed as the final wisdom by so many thinkers. The truth—that love is the ultimate and the highest goal to which man can aspire. Then I grasped the meaning of the greatest secret that human poetry and human thought and belief have to impart: The salvation of man is through love and in love. I understood how a man who has nothing left in this world still may know bliss, be it only for a brief moment, in the contemplation of his beloved. . . . For the first time in my life I was able to understand the meaning of the words, "The angels are lost in perpetual contemplation of an infinite glory."[5]

Frankl would never see his wife again. After being liberated, he managed to pick up the pieces of his life and went on to have a distinguished career, also developing his theory of Logotherapy, which focuses on humankind's search for a higher meaning in life.

The Clash of the Titans

All well and good, Mr. (flip to the front cover) Timothy Dailey, but what does this have to do with the paranormal? More than you might think, as we shall see. Our premise is that a diabolical conspiracy is afoot: a plot to lead human hearts and souls eternally astray. And just as every fisherman needs a lure to make a catch, so does a conspiracy.

To snag his prey, the deceiver works to subvert the only great and wonderful truth that can give ultimate meaning and purpose to the human heart: "God is love."[6]

The conspiracy promises to fulfill that universal, unquenchable yearning for love. Through occult manifestations, it plays upon the heartstrings of its victims, luring them away from the genuine Love they long for and into darkness.

Theologian Francis Schaeffer once remarked that when it comes to the really important questions, there are very few people in the room. When it comes to questions about ultimate meaning and the objective reality of love, the atheist bows out, for such topics have little relevance in a godless universe. That leaves two options—and a philosophical/theological clash between these titans for human allegiance.

The first is the Judeo-Christian worldview, which affirms a universe bursting with meaning and purpose, ruled by a God of love and mercy. The second is the paranormal worldview—belief in a world controlled by unseen forces, variously called "gods," "demons," "spirits" and a multitude of other names across times and cultures.

As Schaeffer noted, paranormal beings are *personal* but not *infinite*, unlike the uniquely personal and infinite God of the Judeo-Christian faith. The paranormal worldview is also one of ambiguity and danger, in which the shaman plays a vital role in appeasing angry and vengeful spirits; the biblical worldview promises government by loving purpose.

This book is an excursion into and exposure of the *Paranormal Conspiracy*—the diabolic plot to overthrow the Judeo-Christian worldview and plunge the world into darkness and chaos not unlike that of the cinematic zombie apocalypse.

The ultimate goal of this cosmic treachery is the destruction of souls, which is warned about in Scripture: "Be alert and of sober mind. Your enemy the devil prowls around like a roaring lion looking for someone to devour."[7] Jesus found Himself in the crosshairs of this infernal plot when the devil approached Him with an offer he was confident the Galilean—weakened after a forty-day fast—could not refuse. After all, did not the Messiah come to govern? *And He shall rule them with a rod of iron*.[8] This the devil offered, with a caveat that seems monstrously arrogant to us: that Jesus should bow the knee and worship him—the archenemy of all that is good. We shall catch glimpses of this imperious vainglory in the stories of those whose lives become entangled with discarnate spirits.

This unearthly impudence is all the more alarming as we witness the formidable power of these mysterious forces that seem to haunt the planet. Is it possible that their enigmatic plans might succeed? Jesus put a swift end to any such speculation with the command that resonates with authority through the ages: "Away from me, Satan! For it is written: 'Worship the Lord your God, and serve him only'"[9] There is no rejoinder; we see nothing of the consummate skills with which—as we shall see—the devil beguiles mortals. Only silence, and instant obedience: "Then the devil left him, and angels came and attended him."[10] What the text leaves unspoken here is the inestimable wrath of a thwarted devil, noted in the book of Revelation: "He is filled with fury, because he knows that his time is short."[11]

Elsewhere Jesus exposes the malignant intent of the devil: "He was a murderer from the beginning, not holding to the truth, for there is no truth in him. When he lies, he speaks his native language, for he is a liar and the father of lies."[12] The devil is aided in this plot by legions of ethereal minions seeking to lead souls astray: "The Spirit clearly says that in later times some will abandon the faith and follow deceiving spirits and things taught by demons."[13]

It should come as no surprise that the central "doctrine of demons" that runs like a thread throughout our exploration is the seductive assurance of the Serpent in the Garden: "You will be like God."[14] The diverse agents of the Paranormal Conspiracy—from the utterances of mediums to the so-called enlightenment of the "exalted masters" to the missives of intergalactic emissaries—all present a cosmology without God at the center. It is a world of their imagining where the Creator has been usurped by His creation, as in William Ernest Henley's defiant "Invictus": *I am the master of my fate, I am the captain of my soul.*

One's destiny in this scheme of things is to toil through the endless transmigration of souls, inhabiting astral realms in between reincarnations until one advances to the level of the "ancient ones" said to have built Atlantis and the pyramids. Then on to the universe beyond—and the fantastically evolved civilizations further along the path of spiritual evolution, the ultimate goal of which is the absorption of one's very personality into the vast Cosmic Sea. And though we shall hear much of "love" on these pages, the Paranormal Conspiracy, in fact, offers a stark universe in which we are completely and utterly alone, destined to lose everything that we know and cherish.

We begin by looking at some influential figures who have popularized this paranormal worldview, including the enigmatic Carlos Castaneda. His experiences with the mysterious shaman don Juan in the deserts of Mexico inspired a generation to seek enlightenment through psychedelics.

The Paranormal Conspiracy seeks to subvert the rational view of the world through mysterious entities that thrive on instability, confusion and fear. Age-old spirit-beasts that inhabit the lonely places—Bigfoot, the Abominable Snow-man et al.—are increasingly making their presence known while maddeningly evading attempts to authenticate their existence. We discover the true source of these phenomena. Similarly, UFO appearances in the skies above defy commonly held theories about their origin, bringing to mind the apostle Paul's reference to "the ruler of the kingdom of the air, the spirit who is now at work in those who are disobedient."[15] We examine the question, Do UFOs originate in the deepest reaches of space—or another dimension?

We then witness Whitley Strieber receiving a harrowing taste of his own medicine when he was abducted from his upstate New York cabin by what appeared to be extraterrestrial aliens. Yet these beings exhibited sadistic cruelty that points to another realm altogether.

Next we visit an unlikely time and place—the heart of the Amazon jungle over a century ago. There we trace the final expedition of intrepid explorer Percy Fawcett, who, like Indiana Jones of the silver screen, sought mystical treasure. Behind the façade of his public persona, we see a life steeped in the esoteric philosophy of Helena Petrovna Blavatsky, called by Kurt Vonnegut "The Founding Mother of the Occult in America."[16] Madame Blavatsky was instrumental in introducing the West to Eastern mysticism, mediumship and occultism.

Following this, we give our attention to the supposed voices of the dead speaking through mediums, and examine the tragic case of journalist Joe Fisher, revealing how deception and perfidy are being cloaked as revelation to a gullible world.

Next we examine how the Paranormal Conspiracy has extended its arcane tentacles to the Internet in the appearance of mysterious, fantastically conceived riddles that have intrigued—and stumped—cyberhackers worldwide. At the deepest levels of the mystery, hackers were surprised to discover the teachings of arch-occultist Aleister Crowley.

And, finally, we examine the enigmatic, shape-shifting trickster who haunts the fringes of human society, and who has alarming connections with the Serpent in the Garden.

Time and again we will witness supposedly evolved beings showering lofty wisdom and grandiose promises on those who fall under their spells. But instead of guiding their "charges" to enlightenment or to mystical promised lands, as the case may be, they plunge them into confusion, despair and, ultimately, terror. We will see that the dark entities, though in possession of unearthly powers, have constraints placed upon them, and may be thwarted entirely by appealing to "the name that is above every name."[17]

Let the journey begin!

THE DOORS OF PERCEPTION

It is a riddle, wrapped in a mystery, inside an enigma—
but perhaps there is a key.

—Winston Churchill, October 1939

n May 1953, *Brave New World* novelist and lifelong student
of mysticism, Aldous Huxley, ingested a dose of the psychedelic drug mescaline, an alkaloid present in the peyote
cactus, at his home in West Hollywood. The eight-hour hallucinogenic trip that followed revealed to him a mesmerizing
world of indescribable beauty and power. The experience
would become the basis for his groundbreaking essay *The
Doors of Perception*,[1] which advocated the use of psychotropic drugs to achieve enlightenment, and the title of which

was taken from William Blake's poetic work *The Marriage of Heaven and Hell*:

> If the doors of perception were cleansed every thing would appear to man as it is, infinite. For man has closed himself up, till he sees all things through narrow chinks of his cavern.

Blake evokes the imagery of Plato's cave, where earthbound souls lie chained in darkness, their vision limited to distorted reflections projected on the walls. Similarly, Huxley believed that true reality lay beyond our normal field of perception, limited as it was by both the mechanistic worldview that denies the existence of spiritual powers and the Christian worldview that warns of their diabolical intent.

Predictably, initial reaction to *The Doors of Perception* was mixed; mostly, though, it was critical of his advocating the use of psychedelic drugs to achieve enlightenment—which for Huxley, long fascinated by Vedantic Hinduism, meant union with the pure consciousness behind the universe called *Brahman*.

After his initial "enlightenment" gained through mescaline, Huxley sought paranormal experiences. He was now convinced that our individual self-awareness—what we call personality—was but a drop in the vast psychic sea. According to one observer, Huxley met regularly with a group of friends who explored "Scientology, animal magnetism, ESP, tele-kinesis, psychic prediction, séances, and other 'mumbo jumbo.'"[2] Transcending one's self to commune with ultimate spiritual reality was, for Huxley, humankind's supreme goal.

Huxley deepened his involvement with psychotropic drugs. Two years later, an experiment with LSD overshadowed even his "doors of perception" revelations. In a letter to a friend he wrote of having realized "the direct, total awareness, from the inside, so to say, of Love as the primary and fundamental cosmic fact." It seems not to have occurred to Huxley that this powerful apprehension of a universe suffused with love necessitated a Lover, and had more in common with biblical theism than Eastern mysticism.

Perhaps it was Huxley's haunting perception of a great love behind the universe that moved him years later as he lay dying to seek it through drugs one last time. Unable to speak, he scribbled a note to his attending wife with the instructions: "LSD, 100 µg, intramuscular." She complied, and followed with another a few hours later in hopes that her beloved Aldous would come to his eternal rest in the arms of the love he had long sought.

A Culture Absorbs the Impact

Aldous Huxley stood on the cusp of a cultural transformation that would soon break out upon the American landscape. He had profound influence upon Beat Generation writers including William Burroughs and Jack Kerouac. Jim Morrison's band, The Doors, which provided a musical score for the counterculture movement, took its name from Huxley's book.

Harvard psychologist Timothy Leary also took inspiration from the book, which affirmed his own experimentation with psychedelic mushrooms and LSD. He would spend the rest of his life championing the hallucinogenic drugs that he described as "the spiritual equivalent of the hydrogen bomb."

In 1967 Leary spoke to a gathering of thirty thousand hippies in San Francisco's Golden Gate Park, where he coined the phrase *Turn on, tune in, drop out*. Much of the country looked askance at the unkempt hippies gathering on the streets of San Francisco; it was almost impossible to comprehend that these idealistic, bell-bottomed young people were the vanguard of a cultural revolution.

Within the hippie movement itself, the early days were not all peace signs and "love-ins." In *Turn Off Your Mind*, Gary Lachman chronicles the dark side of the Age of Aquarius:

> In the 1960's magic, mysticism, and unorthodox forms of spirituality had suddenly taken center stage. Everyone from anonymous hippies on the street to the most famous people in the world, took a trip through the looking glass . . . in the form of meditation, tantric yoga, witchcraft or one of the other weird manifestations of the irrational that saturated the popular consciousness.[3]

You Can Never Go Home Again

Amidst the euphoric rush to cast aside the beliefs and mores that had governed Western thought for centuries—nay, millennia—few noticed that the shining pathway to the new enlightenment was instead a subterfuge. Ironically for many, opening the "doors of perception" led not to peace and love, but to profound spiritual alienation.

The warning signs were nowhere clearer than in the writings of Carlos Castaneda, whose books on his shamanistic experiences sold 28 million copies in seventeen languages.

Castaneda, a graduate student in the field of anthropology at the University of California, Los Angeles, rocketed to fame with *The Teachings of Don Juan: A Yaqui Way of Knowledge*.[4] It came at the height of the countercultural movement. The book and those that followed from his pen became field manuals for the hippie generation that was sprawling out of San Francisco's Haight-Ashbury district and seeking to "turn on" to psychedelics in hopes of achieving enlightenment.

Aldous Huxley was one of Castaneda's favorite authors, but, unlike both Huxley and Leary, he believed that one must master shamanistic practices to use in conjunction with the hallucinogenic peyote, if one were to achieve spiritual advancement. Castaneda came to this persuasion after an arduous, years-long initiation in Mexico at the hands of a mysterious white-haired shaman by the name of don Juan Matus.

The bizarre experiences related by Castaneda in his books strain credulity. Under the tutelage of Matus, and doubtlessly influenced by the peyote, Castaneda claimed to converse with animals and be transformed into a crow. He described careening down a mountainside at breakneck speed while blindfolded, growing a beak and learning to fly. At times Matus appears as Castaneda's friend and mentor, earning the young man's profound respect and admiration—only to turn and reveal the steel heart of a master shaman who intimidates and humiliates his bewildered apprentice.

Castaneda withstood what some would call spiritual abuse at the hands of Matus, returning again and again to the forlorn landscape of the Sonoran Desert, his hoped-for enlightenment always just out of reach. Equally devastating was his realization that after all the peyote ingested, and all the disorienting and frightening spiritual exercises endured, the promised metamorphosis would cut him off forever from everything he knew and loved.

Castaneda shared this epiphany in a haunting passage at the end of his third book, *Journey to Ixtlan: The Lessons of Don Juan*.[5] Don Juan, fellow shaman and friend don Genaro, and Castaneda hiked into the desert and sat together at the top of a hill. There don Genaro related the story of his first encounter with his "ally" or spirit guide.

While on his way home after working in the fields, the young farmer was accosted by a mysterious and powerful being. Suddenly a terrified Genaro was in a life-or-death struggle with the ally, who with a stupendous leap transported Genaro spinning through the air to an unknown destination. Little did the young man realize that his life as a simple farmer, living with his peasant family in the village of Ixtlan, had forever ended.

A disoriented Genaro found himself in unfamiliar surroundings. He started along a path he hoped would lead back to Ixtlan, but everything was different in some inexplicable way. Genaro soon came across travelers along the path who appeared to be Mazatec Indians like himself. They tried to persuade Genaro to join them, but he soon realized that they were deceptive otherworldly beings seeking to mislead him and cause him to trip over the precipices.

Castaneda, struggling to find a rational explanation for what he was hearing, was eager to learn the end of the story. He was informed curtly by don Juan: "There was no final outcome to Genaro's journey. There will never be any final outcome. Genaro is still on his way to Ixtlan!"

Don Genaro glanced at Castaneda with piercing eyes before looking away into the distance, lost in his thoughts:

"I will never reach Ixtlan," he said. His voice was firm but soft, almost a murmur. "Yet in my feelings . . . in my feelings sometimes I think I'm just one step from reaching it. Yet I never will. In my journey I don't even find the familiar landmarks I used to know. Nothing is any longer the same."

Don Juan and don Genaro looked at each other. There was something so sad about their look.

Don Juan then reminded Castaneda that he was on the same shamanistic journey, and that he, like don Genaro, could never go home again:

"As is natural to all of us, the first thing you will want to do is to start on your way back to Los Angeles. But there is no way to go back to Los Angeles. What you left there is lost forever. . . . Yet the feelings in a man do not die or change, and the sorcerer starts on his way back home knowing that he will never reach it, knowing that no power on earth, not even his death, will deliver him to the place, the things, the people he loved."

But Castaneda could not accept this, the loss of everything he knew and loved. Surely there was some way to preserve the links to one's familiar life? Don Juan was unmoved by sentimental appeals:

"Genaro left his passion in Ixtlan: his home, his people, all the things he cared for. And now he wanders around in his feelings; and sometimes, as he says, he almost reaches Ixtlan. All of us have that in common. For Genaro it is Ixtlan; for you it will be Los Angeles; for me. . . ." I did not want don Juan to tell me about himself. He paused as if he had read my mind. Genaro sighed and paraphrased the first lines of the poem. "I left. And the birds stayed, singing." For an instant I sensed a wave of agony and an indescribable loneliness engulfing the three of us.

With that, Matus and Genaro got up and walked back, leaving Castaneda to confront his own ally. Unsettled by what he had just heard, Castaneda realized he was not yet ready for his initiation into shamanism, and decided to return to Los Angeles. But the lure of esoteric knowledge and power that transcends ordinary existence proved too strong, and Castaneda would return to his shamanistic quest.

As Castaneda's own journey to Ixtlan beckoned, don Juan instructed him to "erase his personal history" and sever all human relationships. One of those abandoned for the sorcerer's life was his wife, Margaret, whom he had married in January 1960.

In her memoir, *My Magical Journey with Carlos Castaneda*, she recalled the moment he won her heart: "Carlos looked at me with those big brown eyes that looked like ebony almonds. He was in an impish mood. He whispered, 'Oh, Missa Runyan, I will start a revolution that will last beyond our lifetime—and you are a part of it!'"[6]

But now the desert beckoned:

> The Indians called it becoming a man of knowledge. . . .
> Though he never says so in his books, he actually separated
> from me in September 1960, left many of his friends, began
> keeping irregular hours, missed appointments at UCLA and
> elsewhere and began spending more time in Mexico.[7]

Then the unexpected happened: *The Teachings of Don Juan* became a raging success, catapulting Castaneda to wealth and fame. He retreated to a life of solitude in familiar territory, purchasing a large home in Westwood, California, near UCLA.

Castaneda shared his residence with three elusive women who also cut off all ties with family and friends, joining him in a secretive, cultlike association. Castaneda and this inner circle of followers—self-described witches—refused to be photographed and rarely appeared in public. This fueled the skeptics who alleged that don Juan, as well as many of the events in the books that had introduced so many to shamanism, were little more than a figment of Castaneda's fertile imagination.[8] Undeterred, he continued churning out sequels, but the bloom was off. Years would pass with little of note from the recluse.

Margaret returned home to West Virginia, but what she called her "magical journey" with Castaneda would never end. She continued to refer to their "spiritual marriage," and there were glimmers that Castaneda himself rued the loss of true love:

> In August 1967, he wrote to me: "I went back to your old apt. in the Valley a couple of days [ago] and got an attack of profound sentimentalism. You are my family dearest, dearest Margarita. I felt that as I drove away. What emptiness you have left in my soul! It is the emptiness of losing something irreplaceable."[9]

Decades later, Margaret found herself back in Los Angeles and decided to attempt to make contact. She spotted Castaneda exiting a vehicle and tried to approach, but could not make her way through the cadre of female guardians encircling him. Finally he saw her, waved her over and greeted her warmly. She asked him to autograph her copy of his latest book, but he demurred: "Oh, my hands are too tired." Kissing her on the cheek, he turned and was gone. That was the last time she saw him.

In the words of one reviewer:

> There is a pathetic sadness underlying Margaret's story that probably has its origin in Castaneda's grandiose promises of affection, and his habitual refusal to keep them—coupled with Margaret's steadfast belief in the mystical significance of her life with him.[10]

Castaneda reemerged in the 1990s touting his new "Tensegrity" seminars, which taught shamanistic techniques and promised vibrant good health along with enlightenment. The workshops, which came at a base price of six hundred dollars, pitched Castaneda's books and sold T-shirts emblazoned with the words *The Magic Is in the Movement.*

But it was too late for Castaneda, who was already dying of liver cancer. The end came on April 27, 1998, at his home in Westwood surrounded by his witch companions and an odd assortment of hangers-on. Congruent with the obsessive secrecy with which he lived after returning from his mystical experiences in the Sonoran Desert, news about his death was not made public for a full two months.

A disturbing dark side to Carlos Castaneda's life came to light shortly after his death, when it was discovered that four of his closest disciples had disappeared. The body of one was later recovered in the desert; no trace of the others was ever found. Soon his followers became embroiled in a fight over his estate. Reflecting on Castaneda's troubled legacy, the *New York Times* commented: "His followers say he left the earth with the same elegant, willful mystery that characterized his life. The man he used to call his son says Castaneda died while a virtual prisoner of cultlike followers who controlled his last days and his estate."[11]

It seems that don Juan—whether real or a figment of Castaneda's imagination—was accurate when he told Castaneda that once he crossed the threshold to the shamanistic way of life, he would not be going home again. Though the young man did return to his old haunts in Los Angeles, he was not, and would never again be, the same person. In the end, as noted by the *Times*, "Carlos Castaneda's life and work played out in a wispy blur of sly illusion and artful deceit."

One last intriguing question remains: Did Castaneda's opening of his "doors of perception" and surrendering to the demon-haunted world of the shaman—which we are here calling the Paranormal Conspiracy—instead deceive him into pursuing a hopeless quest that forever separated him from all that he knew and loved?

3

BEINGS OF HIGH STRANGENESS

The Devil and his demons can, according to the literature, manifest themselves in almost any form and can physically imitate anything from angels to horrifying monsters with glowing eyes. Strange objects and entities materialize and dematerialize in these stories.

—John Keel

When science teacher Thom Powell moved to Oregon, he was a typical skeptic regarding the cryptids rumored to inhabit the remote forests of the Pacific Northwest. In class he poked fun at his students' allegations, citing folklore and pseudoscience. Powell was taken aback, however, when neighbors in casual conversation began mentioning the numerous Bigfoot sightings in the area.

His curiosity piqued, Powell decided to conduct his own investigation for the elusive Bigfoot—known alternately as Sasquatch (northwest U.S. and Canada), Skunk Man (or Swamp Ape in Florida, North Carolina and Arkansas) and Yeti (or Abominable Snowman in the Himalayas).

Determined to obtain evidence of the elusive creatures—whatever they proved to be—Powell traveled alone one evening a hundred miles from his home in order to run an experiment in a forest said to be frequented by Bigfoot. Whenever he heard a strange noise and oriented his cameras in that direction, the sound shifted around and came from another direction. His experiment indicated to Powell that the creatures—he was certain this was not human interference—were deliberately avoiding his cameras. They seemed to be responding to him and his equipment in a way that no brute beast would.

Prior to this evening, Powell had learned that members of the Bigfoot Field Researchers Organization (BFRO) suggest that one of the most effective means for attracting a Bigfoot is to make a knocking sound by hitting a board against a tree trunk. Powell whacked away on tree trunks all night long without results. He finally gave up at the crack of dawn and began the two-hour drive back home.

No sooner had Powell pulled into his driveway, parked his car and gotten out than he heard an unmistakable noise coming from the nearby woods. It shook him to his core. It was the same *whack whack whack* sound of a board being hit against a tree trunk that he had made all night long in a forest two hours away.

"The repercussions of that were obvious—that somebody was messing with me," remarked Powell. "I thought I was being the experimenter—and the table just turned."[1] He joined the thousands of ordinary citizens all over the world who have experienced something they cannot explain but attribute to the phenomenon known as Bigfoot.

We see in Powell's experience the mysterious characteristic of Bigfoot sightings: The phenomenon is *unfathomable*—it defies rational understanding and categorization. At first glance, the evidence for the existence of an as-yet undiscovered primate species appears compelling. True believers point to the large numbers of sightings of creatures that fit the description of a large hairy bipedal primate. The BFRO, for example, lists more than 3,300 sightings in its database.[2]

Even more significant, these do not come from snickering high school kids phoning the local police station on a dare. Far from it. Most reports are made by reputable members of the community, including law enforcement officers, teachers and business owners—in short, individuals who have nothing to gain by going public with a Bigfoot sighting.

But is there evidence to back up this impressive body of eyewitness testimony? Those who believe in the existence of Sasquatch answer in the affirmative.

Bigfoot vs. Bili

Bigfoot researchers point to the discovery of a new species of ape in central Africa as proof that large undiscovered primates can exist on the planet.[3] In 2003, *National Geographic* reported that evidence pointing to the existence of an "elusive" population of apes had been discovered near the town of Bili deep within the Democratic Republic of the Congo. The as-yet-unobserved apes were believed to possess features characteristic of both gorillas and giant chimpanzees.

Could similar proof of Bigfoot's existence be just around the corner? One Sasquatch advocacy site notes:

> The discovery of the Bili ape should serve as a cautionary tale to the scientific community about dismissing Bigfoot research altogether. If a giant chimpanzee can exist . . . being unknown to science is it not possible for other large primates to exist in the shadows as well? . . . We are on the verge of a discovery that will far exceed the Bili ape.[4]

Impressive argument—or is it? A closer look indicates that the discovery of the Bili ape highlights the weaknesses of the case for Bigfoot.

Foremost—and this is a biggie—the Bili ape has been observed at length. Reports of the ape date back almost a century. Finally, in 2004, primatologists from the University of Amsterdam undertook an expedition into the heart of the Congo, where they were able to locate and observe the primates continuously for some twenty hours. They took photographs and collected DNA samples, which affirmed the classification of the apes in the chimp subspecies, *Pan troglodytes schweinfurthii.*[5]

According to African wildlife photographer Karl Ammann, the field data "included 12 contacts with the chimpanzees in the study area, a contact being defined as a period of time where the chimpanzees and the observers are aware of one another." In addition, "the winter 2004 update represents daten taken through December 2004 [including] 40 days of collection and many contacts."[6]

Additional study was undertaken by University of Amsterdam researchers in 2006 and 2007. A base camp was established in the Gangu Forest in proximity to the habitat of the Bili apes. Further evidence was collected, including data about their nests and diet. Ammann was able to obtain numerous photographs of the apes, including captured and dead specimens, as well as photographs of primitive tools used by the apes, hair samples and feces.

And Bigfoot? By comparison—well, there is no comparison. The evidence gathered to date falls far short of establishing the existence of Sasquatch—or Yeti or the Skunk Man. Plaster castings of supposed footprints are of dubious value. Even if they proved to be authentic the sheer variety of size and shape—ranging from three to six toes, for instance—would suggest the existence of dozens of highly variant species. The few photographs and video recordings of the creatures—invariably of poor quality—do little to help prove their existence.

The Problems Add Up

Researchers have been trying for more than half a century to prove that Bigfoot exists. After large footprints were discovered at Bluff Creek, California, in 1958, the first hunts for the creature were organized. Interest intensified a decade later with the appearance of the Patterson-Gimlin film, shot at the same location, which we will discuss in a moment.

In spite of the many thousands of Bigfoot sightings across the continental United States and Canada, joined by appearances of similar creatures in other parts of the world, skeptics raise legitimate questions about its existence.

Don't Primates Live in Groups?

Even groups of relatively rare mammals such as chimpanzees require respectable numbers to survive. Large primates, such as great apes, "live in family groups of usually 5 to 10, but sometimes two to more than 50."[7] According to the Cockroach Distribution Theory, if you see one, a dozen more are hiding.

Discovery News points out regarding Bigfoot: "For that population to be big enough to account for even a fraction of the sightings, there would need to be tens of thousands of the creatures in North America alone."[8] Benjamin Radford, editor of *Skeptical Inquirer*, states: "Think about that for a second. Tens of thousands of Bigfoot, living, breathing, doing what they do. Where are they? Why don't they get hit by a car? The numbers just simply don't add up."[9]

Can Primates Hide Their Existence?

Large primates also leave unmistakable traces behind. According to a report by the International Union for Conservation of Nature (IUCN): "Indicators of the presence and abundance of great apes include direct observations, nests, dung, feeding remains, tools, footprints, vocalizations, carcasses."[10]

So why has no physical evidence of Bigfoot been discovered? The most plausible reason given by scientists and laymen who support the phenomenon is that Bigfoot is adept at hiding from humans.

But this borders on the impossible. Great apes are similarly notoriously shy and elusive, yet leave traces of their habitation. The IUCN notes:

Weaned individuals of all great ape species build nests in which they sleep at night or sometimes rest during the day. Nests can remain visible in the forest for several weeks or months after construction and use. Therefore they are encountered at much higher rates than the apes themselves.[11]

Furthermore, apes and other large primates are migratory; proof of their existence is being created continually. Gorillas, for example, construct fresh nests each night. The presence of primate dung at nesting sites allows researchers to determine the age-sex composition of the group and its diet, as well as extract DNA.

It is telling that even *purported* Bigfoot dwelling sites are such a rarity that the Bigfoot Field Research Organization was reduced to posting an article about an "alleged Sasquatch nest."[12] In contrast to great ape nesting sites, which yield clear and abundant evidence of primate activity, the article noted that "all the interior layers were examined for the presence of bone, teeth, hairs, blood, or any other nonorganic materials. No items that could be associated with Sasquatch were found."[13] The BFRO could only conclude: "Since a Sasquatch was not directly observed either making or using the nest, a direct association cannot be made."[14]

What about Their Remote Habitats?

Still, could not the vast, remote wilderness areas where Bigfoot is said to reside offer protection from contact with humans?

Not if we consider that researchers were able to locate the Bili ape deep in the heart of the largest country in sub-Saharan Africa, fully half again the size of Alaska. The search was a logistical nightmare for the University of Amsterdam team. It required a grueling 25-mile trek—including navigating crocodile-invested rivers—off an already primitive path.

By comparison, a distribution map of Sasquatch sightings and population density in each U.S. county reveals that many sightings occur in fairly populated areas.[15] While the geography and topography of some regions—eastern Washington state and Oregon, for example—offer more opportunities for Bigfoot to hide, other regions with high numbers of sightings are relatively flat with few dense forests.

One improbable hot spot for sightings is northeast Ohio. While largely rural, the area is studded with towns and offers a good road system throughout. "Squatching" is an easy day trip from Cleveland. With so many Bigfoot sightings in this highly accessible area, one would expect an abundance of physical evidence, but this is not the case.

What about Search Teams?

A further argument for the existence of Sasquatch is the suggestion that no organized scientific expedition has ever looked for it.

Currently many national, state and regional organizations that search for Bigfoot are active in the United States. The BFRO, founded in 1995, coordinates Bigfoot searches on an annual basis, with some fourteen setting out in 2014 alone. The expeditions target locales in the U.S. and elsewhere that are known for Sasquatch sightings.

The popular Animal Planet television show *Finding Bigfoot* follows the field expeditions of a group of researchers led by BFRO head Matt Moneymaker. A typical episode begins with the team on location to investigate a promising sighting. Witnesses are interviewed and plans are made to reconnoiter for a night observation. The team then employs various strategies to provoke a response from a Bigfoot, including "Squatch calling," tree knocks, baiting and broadcasting recordings of animal sounds. Often a team member will embark upon a solo camping outing in hopes of encountering Bigfoot.

Typically, during the night, the investigating team hears an unidentifiable sound that is taken as a response to their calls. Sometimes an indistinct form, which turns out to be a recognizable animal, appears briefly before their night-vision cameras. On occasion they examine footprints attributed to Sasquatch.

As yet no Bigfoot specimens have been caught on film. Nor have nests or dung been discovered. Still, the show typically concludes with the team high-fiving one another for another successful investigation.

Regarding research teams, we might also note that a number of reputable scientific surveys investigating various other species have been conducted in wilderness areas that would likely have stumbled upon evidence for any new species of large primate.

From 2002 to 2009, for example, numerous teams of biologists under the auspices of Cornell University and other institutions conducted extensive searches for the elusive ivory-billed woodpecker in Arkansas, Louisiana and Florida. Radford notes: "There was a huge, hardcore investigation. They were well-equipped, well-funded and made a sustained search. What I found interesting was, what didn't they find? They didn't find Bigfoot."[16]

The Patterson-Gimlin Film

If we are going to compare Bigfoot to Bili, we have to ask: If primates live together in large numbers, if residue from their habitations is inevitable and if primatologists can find the Bili ape in the vast jungles of the Congo, then why do we continue to lack scientifically validated evidence of Bigfoot? Undeniably, there is an aura of mystery around Bigfoot. This is the perfect breeding ground for anyone who wants to take advantage of an opportunity for personal gain or simply amusement. More than one jokester has confessed to tramping through the forest and making impressions in the ground with wooden forms of very large feet.

I mentioned earlier that photographs and films of Bigfoot are typically poor—unsteady shots of a large, dark fleeing creature. The film versions last no more than a few seconds—except for one much-publicized video image that is cited as proof of the existence of Bigfoot.

Here is the story in a nutshell: A known con man sets out to create a Bigfoot documentary and—lo and behold!—on his very first outing he succeeds in capturing Sasquatch on film.

This summarizes the Coincidence of the Century that is the Patterson-Gimlin film. In October 1967, at Bluff Creek in northern California, Roger Patterson and his friend Bob Gimlin claimed to have filmed a female Bigfoot striding purposefully into the woods and turning her head to glance at them over her shoulder. The 16mm film has been analyzed endlessly. Experts either swear by or denounce the authenticity of the 53 seconds of grainy footage—an eternity for a Bigfoot sighting.

Lost amidst the frame-by-frame scrutiny is the fact that Patterson is a poster child for the truism *Consider the source*.

Despite intense interest in the film, surprisingly little was known about the man—until Greg Long laid it all out in his 2004 book, *The Making of Bigfoot: The Inside Story*.[17] Long spent years tracking down anyone and everyone who had anything to do with Patterson, and the portrait he paints is not flattering. Patterson played for a sucker almost everyone he knew, from his best friends to his own mother. If there is one criticism of the author's efforts, it is that the book is too repetitive. It chronicles the words of witness after witness heaping scorn upon Patterson. One summarizes him as "a cheat, a liar, and a thief."

Where to begin? The man held more jobs than an incurable flatulent. At various and sundry times he was a woodworker, artist, acrobat, rodeo-rider, writer, filmmaker—but, above all, a con man. It was in pursuit of this last vocation that Patterson, long fascinated with the Bigfoot legend, apparently dreamed up a scheme to build interest in a documentary on the subject.

To persuade his contacts in Hollywood to sign on the dotted line, all he needed was some footage of the creatures. As Bigfoot skeptic Joe Nickell notes, the "female creature's general appearance, pendulous breasts, and bent-knee walk were just as Patterson the artist had illustrated in his book the year before."[18] The rest, as they say, is history.

If we set aside the Patterson-Gimlin film, Bigfoot advocates are left with meager pickings indeed. Aside from questionable footprints, it is as if every camera used to capture Bigfoot was jostled so as to leave us with nothing but dark blurs. A proper flash would do wonders for nighttime shots of Bigfoot.

To my knowledge, the public has never seen a single, clear, unambiguous photo or film of a Bigfoot. We shall presently see that Bigfoot is not the only phenomenon characterized by reliable eyewitnesses, yet—mysteriously—with an almost complete lack of empirical evidence.

The Witnesses Speak

Where does this leave the sincere individual—each one of those thousands—who is convinced that he or she encountered something real and who is looking for validation? Let's return for a moment to the *Finding Bigfoot* television program. The most compelling segment of the episodes, and one that rings with authenticity, is the "town hall meeting." This is the heart of the program. The investigators, arriving in different locales, invite all those who have had unexplainable encounters to share their experiences, which then guide the team's search efforts.

These town hall meetings give voice to ordinary citizens who have observed *something* that challenged their assumptions about the world around them. Those who testify come from all walks of life, and their stories give no indication of being scripted or prompted by the research team. All they stand to gain for claiming to see large hairy bipeds is the loss of standing in their community and the ridicule of friends and family.

Granted, an eyewitness account cannot be observed under a laboratory microscope. And, unquestionably, memory can be faulty, incomplete or influenced by leading questions. But, nonetheless, eyewitness testimony plays an important role in our lives. The criminal justice system is one important example. In a thousand different ways, great and small, much of our daily routine relies on access to personal recollection.

Certainly the possibility exists that some sightings are deliberate hoaxes. Others may well be misidentifications of, say, a bear. But it defies both logic and common sense to dismiss such a large body of eyewitness testimony.

Enter UFOs

Renowned UFO researcher and Air Force Project Blue Book advisor J. Allen Hynek referred to this kind of testimony as "credible persons reporting incredible things." The parallel of UFOs to Bigfoot is substantial, and the lines between them are beginning to intersect. Here is an eyewitness account that helps us begin to decipher what is going on with strange sightings that leave no physical evidence.

Mrs. Han lives deep in the woods of rural Fayette County, Pennsylvania, just across the state line from the aforementioned Bigfoot hot spot in northeast Ohio.[19] But she has never paid any mind to such things. Then, around ten p.m. one night, just as she was getting ready for bed, Mrs. Han heard a commotion in her front yard. Thinking that wild dogs were coming around, she chambered a round in her 16-gauge shotgun and opened the front door to give them a welcome they would not soon forget.

Even now, decades later, the fright she experienced when she stepped out onto her porch is indelibly etched in her mind. Standing in the middle of her yard almost within spitting distance was a massive hairy creature. Mrs. Han did not hesitate. Opting instinctively for the *fight* option of "fight or flight," she raised her shotgun and fired at close range.

What happened then illustrates the mysterious nature of a surprising number of Bigfoot sightings: The creature disappeared. Not "disappeared" as in "ran away quickly," but "disappeared" as in "*poof*—it was gone!"

Her son, who lived nearby, heard the commotion and came running out with his handgun. Seeing shadowy creatures off in the darkness and sensing danger, he fired at them. Then Mrs. Han and her son witnessed another mystifying aspect of the Bigfoot phenomena that is rarely mentioned by Bigfoot researchers: They saw UFO-like lights in the sky, which Mrs. Han's son described as large Christmas tree ornaments. He ran to call the police, but by the time the officers arrived there was no sign of creature or craft.

The bizarre experience of Mrs. Han and her son is by no means unique. Veteran paranormal researcher Stan Gordon became aware of unusual phenomena while investigating a series of UFO sightings in Pennsylvania:

> Among the oddities reported were cases where both a UFO and a Bigfoot were observed at the same time and place. In one case, a UFO was observed on or near the ground and two Bigfoot creatures were observed in the same field. After the object departed and the creatures went into the woods, a state trooper who came to the scene to investigate observed a glowing area on the ground where the object had rested a short time before. . . . It soon became apparent to myself and other investigators that there were other aspects to the Bigfoot phenomena that could not be ignored.[20]

The Inhumanoids

And so the debate continues between two intractable positions. On the one hand, Bigfoot believers insist that a flesh-and-blood descendant of *Gigantopithecus* is roaming the planet. They hold their ground even though the case for a literal Bigfoot, as we have seen, is hampered by the lack of physical proof.

On the other hand, skeptics point to that lack of hard evidence: "Bigfoot? Prove it!" But the critics are not on such firm ground either, as we have also seen, for their position requires them to discount a very large and impressive body of reliable witnesses—including police officers and other professionals who are trained to report their observations accurately.

The lack of physical evidence for an occurrence that is experienced visually opens the way for a third possibility—one that, oddly, is anathema to both sides of the debate. This suggestion is a trans-physical or interdimensional origin of creatures that are able temporarily to intersect our world. Bigfoot enthusiasts reject this idea because they have sought scientific respectability too long and hard to throw it all away with a spiritualistic explanation. Skeptic materialists, meaning those who reject the possibility of the supernatural, reject it because they pride themselves in not admitting the existence of anything that cannot be measured scientifically.

Is a metaphysical explanation plausible? It certainly becomes more attractive once the worldwide range of such phenomena is considered. Bigfoot is only one of a wild assortment of mysterious cryptids roaming the planet, from Chupacabra to Mothman, Dover Demon to Jersey Devil, Goatman to Hellhound—and a myriad of others.

The sightings of all these different creatures share common features. Suddenly someone feels the instinctual fear of mortal danger—a brute animal stalks. The beast is spotted—only a glimpse before it retreats into the shadows. A photo might be taken, but it is only a glancing shot. The witnesses might be unimpeachable—but there is little to offer as proof save a chilling realization that, in the words of Macbeth, something wicked this way comes.

Not every researcher, of course, is shielding his eyes to the possibility of otherworldly manifestations on earth. Kentucky Bigfoot researcher and author Barton Nunnelly has a word for this type of creature: *inhumanoid*:

> I believe all unexplained, man-like creatures to be fundamentally related, including Bigfoot. Many of them share eerily similar characteristics and [elicit] the exact same response in witnesses. From my own experiences I can tell you that there is definitely more to these creatures than many researchers are prepared to admit. My simplified answer would be that these are supernatural entities which can appear as whatever they wish to.[21]

Similarly, Stan Gordon reports that many Bigfoot sightings are accompanied by phenomena traditionally associated with demonic activity, such as the stench of sulphur or rotten meat. Researchers also notice that domestic and farm animals react with inordinate fear during sightings: "It was very significant in dogs that were in close range to a Bigfoot. Even the most ferocious dogs wouldn't bark, became still or shaken, and hid in their cages or under dwellings. In some cases they wouldn't eat normally for days later."[22]

Like Mrs. Han and her son, researchers are increasingly looking to the sky and realizing the connection between cryptids and UFOs. The appearance of both phenomena together indicates a symbiotic relationship, with mysterious cryptids sowing fear and confusion and serving to disrupt our ordered conception of the world. Could these "inhumanoid" entities be preparing the way for a techno-occult variation appearing in the heavens as fantastically advanced spaceships—proclaiming a New Age formulation of the primordial lie "You will be like God"? We will now consider the staggering implications of just such a possibility.

MESSENGERS OF DECEPTION

UFOs could well be part of the same larger intelligence which has shaped the tapestry of religion and mythology since the dawn of human consciousness.

—J. Allen Hynek

The news broke across the nation like a shot in the darkness. Radar on U.S. Navy vessels in the North Atlantic had detected an unidentified craft flying at supersonic speeds toward the East Coast of the United States—on a flight path to the nation's capital. Military assets scarcely had time to respond before the silver disk glided to a stop on the grassy National Mall in Washington, D.C., near the White House.

A panel on the craft slid open, and a solemn humanlike being emerged bearing a message for the leaders of the world.

47

After observing the development of atomic power on earth, the inhabitants of distant planets had grown concerned for their own safety: "If you threaten to extend your violence," the alien emissary warned, "this earth of yours will be reduced to a burned out cinder. Your choice is simple: Join us and live in peace, or pursue your present course and face obliteration."

By now science fiction *aficionados* are mouthing the dialogue of actor Michael Rennie as "Klaatu" in the 1951 science fiction classic, *The Day the Earth Stood Still*. The critically acclaimed production was one of the first of many science fiction films to thrill moviegoers.

In a bizarre case of life imitating art, less than a year after the film's release, Washington, D.C., was visited by what had come to be termed Unidentified Flying Objects. In 1952, the "Washington flap" centered on a series of UFO sightings that began late on the night of July 19 when an air traffic controller at Washington National Airport (now Ronald Reagan Washington National Airport) spotted seven curious blips on his radar screen. He alerted his supervisor, who determined that the radar unit was operating properly and discovered that a second radar center at the airport had also recorded the presence of the unknown craft. Radar operators on two military air bases in the area, Andrews and Bolling Air Force bases, had also seen the blips.[1]

The objects were on a trajectory identical to that of Klaatu's craft, taking them directly over the White House and the U.S. Capitol. F-94 Starfires were scrambled to meet the threat. And then things began to get strange.

The pilots reported that as their jets raced to intercept the lights, the UFOs blacked out—only to reappear when the Air

Force jets, low on fuel, were forced to return to base. Over the next several hours a cat-and-mouse game was played out in the skies over Washington, with the UFOs making sudden, gut-wrenching changes of direction impossible for any known aircraft, and shooting away at fantastic speeds. At one point, a UFO that was being tracked by three airport traffic centers disappeared from each of the radars simultaneously, prompting one senior air traffic controller to speculate that "the UFOs were monitoring radio traffic and behaving accordingly."[2] A week later, as if on cue, the UFOs returned for an encore performance.

Pressed for an explanation, an Air Force spokesman suggested that the sightings could be explained by temperature inversion, an atmospheric condition that traps a layer of cold air under a layer of warm air. Light is refracted, causing objects near the ground to appear as if they are high in the sky.

UFO researchers scoff at this, pointing out that the same temperature inversion conditions had existed throughout the summer—without causing the appearance of strange flying objects in the sky and on radar. One UFO organization concluded:

The Washington D. C. sightings are a solid case of UFO activity. Literally hundreds of eyewitnesses saw the objects, and photographed them. Many of these were Air Force personnel, considered as reliable. Many of them made comment of the sightings, one was a Sergeant Harrison: "I saw the . . . light moving from the Northeast toward the range station. These lights did not have the characteristics of shooting stars. There was no trails and seemed to go out rather than disappear, and traveled faster than any shooting star I have ever seen."[3]

Intergalactic Nuclear Paranoia

One evening in November of the same year, Polish-American émigré George Adamski walked out into the California desert. He returned hours later with a strange tale of having communicated telepathically with Venusian aliens in a translucent metal UFO that descended from the sky.

In his book *Flying Saucers Have Landed*, Adamski claims that extraterrestrials from Venus and other planets in the solar system visit earth regularly. He describes the long-blond-haired "space brother" pilot named "Orthon":

> The beauty of his form surpassed anything I had ever seen. And the pleasantness of his face freed me of all thought of my personal self. I felt like a little child in the presence of one with great wisdom and much love, and I became very humble within myself . . . for from him was radiating a feeling of infinite understanding and kindness, with supreme humility.[4]

Adamski went on to write numerous books on UFOs and gained a cult following even as his story unraveled. For one thing, it was highly unlikely that humanlike aliens could survive on a planet with an average temperature of almost 500 degrees and an atmospheric pressure 92 times that of earth.

Adamski borrowed many of his ideas from the Russian occultist Madame Helena Blavatsky (1831–1891), founder of the Theosophical Society, an esoteric system of philosophy modeled after Eastern mysticism. Blavatsky taught that spiritually advanced creatures on planets such as Venus were instrumental in the evolution of humanity. To her admirers, Blavatsky was considered the High Priestess of Isis, a "Messenger of the Light," or simply "the most remarkable woman of our century." In the late 1920s Adamski and his wife had founded the "Royal Order of Tibet" and set up a commune organized around her teachings.

Though Adamski would be largely discredited, his story contains aspects of the "contactee" experience described in cases of alleged contact with aliens. Adamski's Venusian Orthon, for example, is the prototypical "Nordic" alien type, described as tall with long blond hair and blue eyes. Another common feature of Nordics is that they express concern with the spiritual growth of humankind—and the survival of the planet. As in *The Day the Earth Stood Still*, the purpose of Orthon's extraterrestrial visit was to warn humankind of the inherent folly in building nuclear weapons, which could not only annihilate life on our planet but also threaten other civilizations in outer space. This *Watch out or you'll spoil things for the entire galaxy* theme has become a constant refrain throughout the history of "ufology" (the study of UFOs).

In *UFOs and Nukes: Extraordinary Encounters at Nuclear Weapons Sites*,[5] ufologist Robert Hastings argues that our planet is in for a rude awakening of cosmic proportions when the news finally breaks that aliens from far-flung points in space have been coming around, demanding that we rein in this destructive technology:

> When the Big News finally breaks—when some unimpeach-able, high-level government insider finally admits on-the-record that UFOs are very real and that those who pilot them, although seemingly not from the neighborhood, are nevertheless interested in and apparently concerned about our nuclear weapons—humanity's future will take a dramatic

new turn. . . . Everything we humans thought we knew about reality will be up for grabs.[6]

Ufologists argue that sightings of alien spaceships soared during periods of high levels of nuclear weapon detonations. Since the beginning of the nuclear age there have been tens of thousands of reports of strange, unexplainable objects in the sky. According to Hastings, "If we assume, very conservatively, that one in a hundred of those reports are of bona fide UFOs, that still leaves an awful lot of aerodynamically-anomalous craft operating in our atmosphere, on an ongoing basis."[7]

But does the belief in evolved space aliens visiting earth, first taught by Blavatsky and accepted by many ufologists, square with facts—or is it even possible? Let's look into our "galactic neighborhood."

The Ranges of the Divine

Few of us, perhaps, can begin to imagine moving at the speed of 186,000 miles a second—the speed of light. An hour, day or month of travel at that speed is simply beyond our grasp. The appellation *Milky Way galaxy* rolls off the tongue as if we know of what we speak: Our astronomical home—as it were—is *150,000 light years* in diameter. The Milky Way's nearest sister, the Andromeda Galaxy, is roughly 2.5 million light years away. All told, there are probably more than 100 billion galaxies in the observable universe, which is about *46 billion light years* in radius.[8]

Galaxies can range in size from dwarfs with as few as ten million stars to giants with a trillion stars. And just in case you are not feeling small and negligible enough in the cosmos, the current thinking is that the observable universe might contain as many stars as the number three followed by more than a thousand zeros. For the layman, that means there are up to ten times as many stars as there are grains of sand on all the world's beaches and deserts put together. But we might as well be speaking gibberish, as if there were any meaningful analogy between words like *space* and *distance* and our cosmologically insignificant lives on an infinitesimal planet orbiting one of the estimated four hundred million stars in the Milky Way. It is, however, at this very point that the proffered reason for UFOs journeying to earth from distant galaxies—alarmed at the detonation of atomic weapons—begins to falter, finally collapsing under its own weight.

The Fermi Paradox

At first glance, life on other planets seems eminently reasonable. How can there *not* be life in the vast expanse of the universe? And statistically, at least *some* of those interstellar civilizations would be more advanced than our own, and, thus, would likely have the capability of traversing the universe.

And they would have much to teach us: Any civilization that has managed to exist for millions of years would surely have banished violence and warfare, and would long have mastered the keys to love and ultimate meaning. Adamski was deeply attached to his "space brother" Orthon, writing that "the presence of this inhabitant of Venus was like the warm embrace of great love and understanding wisdom."[9]

Ironically, it was Enrico Fermi—the "father of the atomic bomb"—who, in an offhand remark during a lunchtime conversation, posed a devastating argument against the Extraterrestrial Hypothesis—the theory that UFOs and aliens come from outer space. The eminent Italian physicist and Nobel Laureate played a pivotal role in the first nuclear reactor as well as the development of quantum theory and particle physics.[10] He had the kind of scientific mind that could—and did—build a working atomic reactor in a squash court.

Over lunch one day with his colleagues, the question arose about whether or not the Milky Way galaxy is populated with advanced civilizations. The consensus around the table was that it is reasonable to assume that earth has plenty of cosmic company. The great physicist, however, detected a flaw in that assumption.

During his own lifetime, Fermi noted, he had seen tremendous technological development along with a growing interest in exploring outer space. It is both reasonable and likely, continued Fermi, that any other intelligent civilization in the galaxy would also possess the same curiosity about other possible worlds. In the decades since Fermi's death in 1954, earthlings have walked on the moon, landed rover vehicles on Mars and sent probes to distant parts of the solar system—all reinforcing his argument.

How many other civilizations exist in the Milky Way? Presumably, civilizations evolve on planets, and a recently published evaluation of data from the Kepler Space Observatory by a team of NASA scientists indicates that there are an estimated 8.8 billion earthlike planets in our galaxy.[11] And how many of those planets hold intelligent life?

I will get back to Fermi's argument in a moment. First, let's think about this question of intelligent life. Renowned astrophysicist Frank Drake attempted to answer this question using a method of determining how many intelligent civilizations might have evolved within the Milky Way galaxy. Using the Drake Equation, some astronomers suggest that the estimated number of intelligent civilizations could be in the 10,000 range, a figure confirmed by data provided by NASA's Kepler scientists.

Let's suppose that there are 10,000 civilizations in our galaxy that are advanced enough to emit the kind of radio and electronic signals into space that we earthlings are sending, intentionally or unintentionally.[12] How many of these 10,000 civilizations are capable of sending UFOs to earth? In other words, the critical question is really this: How many of these 10,000 civilizations are *more advanced than earth*?

According to evolutionary cosmology, the Milky Way galaxy is estimated to be *some ten thousand million years old*. Assuming for the sake of argument that this is correct, it would mean that the earth has been around for several billion years. It should then follow that the older parts of our galaxy theoretically contain civilizations that have evolved millions of years beyond our own.

This is a key consideration, for if other inhabited worlds have even the same level of rocket technology developed thus far by *homo sapiens*, they would be able to send probes to other star systems in the galaxy. Given the vast amounts of time these civilizations presumably have had to develop technology, those older than earth by a quantum factor could undoubtedly have developed much more efficient means of propulsion, making it even more likely that we should have been contacted at some point by our galactic neighbors.

It was this inescapable point that Enrico Fermi grasped, for if other advanced civilizations exist, *they would long ago have visited—and very possibly would still be visiting*, and even colonizing and exploiting earth, prompting his question: "Where is everybody?"

Dozens of papers addressing the Fermi Paradox have been published as scientists and UFO researchers study the question of why the intelligent life that is widely believed to exist is silent. Attempts to answer Fermi by "tweaking" the numbers have fallen short, being eclipsed by the immeasurably vast amounts of time, as noted by one commentator:

> You can quibble about the speed of alien spacecraft, and whether they can move at 1 percent of the speed of light or 10 percent of the speed of light. It doesn't matter. You can argue about how long it would take for a new star colony to spawn colonies of its own. It still doesn't matter. Any halfway reasonable assumption about how fast colonization could take place still ends up with time scales that are profoundly shorter than the age of the Galaxy.[13]

A Cosmic Pinprick

Let's take a closer look at the argument that nuclear explosions have drawn the attention of faraway alien civilizations. Little Boy was the code name for the atomic bomb dropped on the Japanese city of Hiroshima on August 6, 1945, exploding with an energy of 16 kilotons of TNT. At the time, Little Boy was by far the most powerful weapon known to mankind, but it would soon be eclipsed. The first liquid deuterium fusion bomb was tested by the United States in 1952 in the Marshall Islands in the central Pacific Ocean. Its explosion yielded an energy equivalent to 10.4 megatons of TNT—more than 450 times the power of the bombs dropped on Hiroshima and Nagasaki.

The Nuclear Arms Race was underway. As a show of political strength, the Soviet Union tested the largest-ever nuclear weapon in October 1961, the massive *Tsar Bomba*, which was estimated to have an explosive force of around 100 megatons—or 4,500 times greater than the now aptly named Little Boy. All told, more than five hundred atmospheric nuclear weapons tests were conducted at various sites around the world from 1945 to 1980.

Our brains struggle to grasp this level of sheer energy and explosive force. Of course! It makes perfect sense, therefore, that alien civilizations, concerned about the hundreds of nuclear explosions in our atmosphere, have come to warn us of the insanity of our ways.

Now let's take a look at a few comparisons that expose the folly of such a notion—for, truly, it rivals the notion that alien civilizations might be equally concerned about the biodiversity of the world's oceans.

First off, the greatest nuclear explosions on the earth are a pinprick compared to what is happening on the sun, which has an energy output roughly equivalent to *one hundred billion nuclear bombs going off every second*. Try not to get hung up on that incomprehensible fact for too long, because the train has not even left the station.

As it turns out, our sun is actually puny compared to some of the behemoth luminaries in the universe. Currently, the most massive star that we know of is a monster called VY Canis Majoris, thought to have a volume that is one billion times that of our sun. Put another way, "it would take over 7,000,000,000,000,000 (7 Quadrillion) Earths or 7,000,000,000 (7 Billion) Suns to fill VY Canis Majoris."[14] The explosions of distant stars, by which they become supernovas, generate an equivalent amount of energy as this massive sun. As the NASA website notes, however: "Even though the explosion [of a supernova] is as bright as a billion suns, it is so far away that it is just a speck of light."[15]

Can you see the supernova-sized problem with the alien-intervention-to-save-the-planet theory? Our sun produces a level of energy *each second* that is the equivalent of one hundred billion nuclear bombs. Megastars and supernovas generate a level of energy that is up to *a billion times greater* than that of our sun. If such gargantuan explosions appear as a mere "pinprick" in space—then it is nothing short of ludicrous to think that aliens would take notice of such infinitesimal (in the grand scheme of things) explosions on our tiny planet hundreds, thousands, even billions of light years away.

And we are not talking about the concern of just *one* alien civilization. The tremendous diversity in the shapes and sizes of UFOs suggests that earth is being visited by hundreds of intergalactic civilizations. Writer Brad Steiger lists some of the most common types of UFOs he has encountered in more than forty years of research: a blinding light; a diamond-shaped or egg-shaped "mother ship"; a boomerang or crescent; a flat-edged coin shape; a football shape; a conical disk; and the classically recognized domed saucer shape complete with "an exhaust port on the bottom

[that] emits a yellow light that dances like a flame upon takeoff," presumably to assist with accelerating the craft to warp speed.[16]

The same bewildering diversity is found in the aliens themselves. In addition to the "Nordic," "grey" and "reptilian" types, witnesses have reported "short, big-headed creatures; human figures; monkey-like aliens; one-eyed monsters; creatures with one leg; creatures with webbed fingers; some speak fluent English, others communicate with grunts and signs, others seem to be telepathic."[17]

In an essay on descriptions of UFO occupants, British paranormal researcher Peter Hough remarks:

> These hundreds of conflicting descriptions weigh heavily against the supposition that many UFOs are spacecraft piloted by extraterrestrial visitors. For this would imply that Earth is some sort of Galactic Mecca for hundreds of different space travelling civilizations . . . with alleged messages on the lines of: "We are aliens from planet X, friendly and concerned for the wellbeing of your world. Stop tinkering with nuclear energy before it is too late."[18]

With a message so crucial, is it not a curious *modus operandi* for the space travelers to slip quickly across the sky, barely seen? All this time and not a single verifiable landing in Washington, D.C., or a state capital, police station, football stadium—there are endless possibilities of where and how the aliens could reveal themselves.

Sometimes we are told that aliens have revealed themselves through chosen human vessels. The message in these cases is suspiciously trendy, and laced with mystical philosophy. With characteristic perspicuity, eminent astronomer Carl

Sagan cuts through the ufologist argument that beings from advanced civilizations have come to warn earthlings:

> How is it, I ask myself, that UFO occupants are so bound to fashionable or urgent concerns on this planet? Why not an incidental warning about CFCs and ozone depletion in the 1950's or about the HIV virus in the 1970's, when it might really have done some good? Why not alert us now to some public health or environmental threat we haven't yet figured out? Can it be that aliens know only as much as those who report their presence? And if one of the chief purposes of alien visitations is admonitions about global dangers, why tell it only to a few people whose accounts are suspect anyway? Why not take over the television networks for a night, or appear with vivid cautionary audiovisuals before the United Nations Security Council? Surely this is not too difficult for those who wing across the light years.[19]

The late Harvard psychiatrist and Pulitzer Prize–winning author, Dr. John Mack, interviewed hundreds of men and women who claimed to have had contact with aliens, and confirmed that a common theme propagated by the entities was pantheistic cosmic consciousness:

> The aliens are recognized as intermediaries or intermediate entities between the fully bodied state of human beings and the primal source of creation or God (in the sense of a cosmic consciousness, rather than a personified being). In this regard abductees sometimes liken the alien beings to angels, or other "light beings" (including the "grays").[20]

Renowned UFO researcher John Keel spent four decades studying the paranormal. His book *The Mothman Prophe-*

cies[21] was the inspiration for the eerie film adaptation starring Richard Gere. He came to suspect a connection between aliens and occultism, and in *Operation Trojan Horse* writes:

> The endless messages from the space people would now fill a library, and while the communicators claim to represent some other world, the contents of those messages are identical to the messages long received by mediums and mystics.[22]

They Love Darkness

Then there is the curious anomaly that so many UFO sightings occur under cover of darkness. Computer scientist and ufologist Jacques Vallée conducted a statistical analysis of UFO sightings and alleged encounters worldwide, which yielded a typical bell curve with the majority of incidents occurring late at night:

> On these curves it can be seen that the number of close encounters is very low during the daylight hours. It starts increasing about five P.M. and reaches a maximum about nine P.M. It then decreases steadily until one A.M., then rises again to a secondary peak about three A.M. and returns to its low diurnal level by six [a.m.].[23]

What are the chances that so many of the alleged spaceships from distant galaxies just happen to make their fleeting appearance in our atmosphere in the dead of night? That, along with the fact that most alien abductions, which we will discuss in the next chapter, also occur during the night indicates a disquieting connection between the UFO phenomenon and darkness, bringing to mind the words of Jesus about those who "loved the darkness rather than the Light, for their deeds were evil. For everyone who does evil hates the Light, and does not come to the Light for fear that his deeds will be exposed."[24]

The apostle Paul warned of dark powers in the heavens: "For our struggle is not against flesh and blood, but against the rulers, against the authorities, against the powers of this dark world and against the spiritual forces of evil in the heavenly realms."[25] Even Keel, who did not write from a religious perspective, came to question the motivations of the aliens, who professed love and concern for humanity: "Do the ultraterrestrials really care about us? There is much disturbing evidence that they don't. They care only to the extent that we can fulfill our enigmatic use to them."[26]

In *Operation Trojan Horse*, Keel concludes that whoever or whatever is behind the UFOs comes not from distant galaxies but from another dimension: "The UFO manifestations seem to be, by and large, merely minor variations of the age-old demonological phenomenon."[27]

If such entities are irremediably evil, then deception and obfuscation are their trademarks. Thus, it is not surprising, as Dr. Karla Turner notes, that conclusive proof of the UFO phenomenon is wanting:

> In spite of half a century of many intelligent people researching the UFO and alien presence with scientific methods, reliable answers to the primary questions have not been found. Investigations of sightings reports, landing traces, photos and video tapes, alleged implants, and related government documents have amassed a mountain of data and a number of theories—but nothing indisputably true about the nature

of UFOs and their non-human occupants, their origin, or the reason for their presence here among us now.[28]

Some ufologists follow Hastings' suggestion that UFOs and alien abductions are intended to transform human society:

> I would argue it seems likely, if not a certainty, that the resolution of the UFO enigma will constitute a bona fide "paradigm shift." These consciousness-raising transformations are rare, but when they occur, human understanding is undeniably advanced in a manner that precludes going back to the previous, collective conception of reality.[29]

Even more troubling, this metamorphosis can forever alter the lives of those who come into contact with these entities. Turner writes:

> And finally there are the internal changes that take place with most abductees, reshaping their attitudes, belief structures, and perceptions of reality. Thus, the externally induced, temporary, altered awareness which occurs during abductions is paralleled by a permanent, internal alteration, and the abductee's life is forever changed.[30]

We will now examine the terrifying consequences suffered by those whose lives are turned upside down after experiencing "aliens" up close and personal.

UNEARTHLY ENCOUNTERS

Far from being a neat, limited phenomenon, alien interaction with humans is still very much a riddle, mystery, enigma, and more.

—Karla Turner

Horror novelist Whitley Strieber was earning a good living creating nightmares. Little did he know that one day an unspeakable terror would literally come calling—and at the most unexpected time and place.

It was Christmas, 1985. Strieber, his wife and young son had retired to their isolated cabin in upstate New York to enjoy a quiet holiday season away from the rat race they call life in the Big Apple. Increasingly concerned about intruders—or perhaps from a foreboding of evil visitation—he had just had an elaborate security system installed in the cabin.

Strieber, admittedly, trafficked in fear. His novels featured the paranormal themes of vampires, werewolves, black magic and witches. In retrospect, the terror that would descend upon Strieber is not entirely surprising given that he has long been trolling in dangerous waters.

A fresh blanket of snow provided a picture-perfect backdrop for an idyllic holiday. The family spent the day sledding and cross-country skiing before enjoying Christmas dinner leftovers of goose, cranberry sauce and sweet potatoes. After tucking their son into bed, Strieber and his wife sat up reading and listening to music. Late in the evening, after Strieber set the alarm, they retired to bed and were soon fast asleep.

But something was lurking outside. As related in his book *Communion*,[1] life was about to come crashing down for Strieber. Curiously, like so many who experience life-shaking trauma, he remembered nothing of that night, waking only to a vague recollection of a nightmare that was receding into his subconscious.

In the days and weeks that followed, however, Strieber noticed a change in his personality. He suffered extreme mood swings and a disturbing paranoia. He also suffered from inexplicable physical discomfort, such as rectal pain and soreness behind his ear, where a small scar was evident.

Strieber contacted artist-turned-abduction-researcher Budd Hopkins, author of *Intruders* and *Missing Time*.[2] Hopkins put Strieber in touch with psychiatrist Donald Klein, who practices hypnotic regression. Under the trained eye of Dr. Klein, the bizarre events of that fateful night in December began to unfold. Far from an isolated incident, they discovered that this was one in a series of otherworldly encounters stretching back to Strieber's childhood.

Under hypnosis, Strieber recalled being jarred awake in the middle of that wintry night. Instantly alert, he listened for sounds, and heard in the living room below the distinct noise of people moving about.

Intruders! You and I can readily imagine how *we* would react: by either catapulting out of bed to confront the threat or squirreling beneath it. Strieber, oddly, did neither: He settled back down.

Then the unthinkable happened: Looking across the dark room Strieber saw the bedroom door opening slowly. He sat bolt upright next to his sleeping wife, his heart pounding. Hoping against hope that it was his son coming to their room after having made a commotion downstairs, he instead sensed an ominous presence and braced himself: "Then I saw edging around [the door] a compact figure. It was so distinct, and yet so impossibly astonishing that at first I could not understand it at all. I simply sat there staring, too stunned to move."[3]

Strieber estimates that the "entity" (for lack of a better term) was about three and a half feet tall and dressed in costume-like clothing. Its nondescript face had "two dark holes for eyes and a black, downturned line of a mouth that later became an 'O.'"[4]

The entity rushed toward an aghast Strieber. What came next beggars description. He was somehow transported out of his bedroom into the woods, where he found himself sitting on the frozen ground. He was powerless to put up the slightest struggle. He could not move any part of his body—except for his eyes.

More entities began swarming around him, drawing closer. One of them was "working busily at something that seemed to have to do with the right side of my head."[5] Strieber learned later that the particular interest being shown to his head was a common feature of what have come to be known as alien abductions, leading some to speculate that the abductee's consciousness is being altered in some unimaginable way.

Strieber's abduction experience was far from over. Next he was transported above the darkened forest into some kind of craft, where he was deposited into a room that was round in shape, unkempt and dirty. What he took to be alien garments were strewn about.

This was no ordinary dream. Every nerve in Strieber's body was throbbing with acute awareness. His growing sense of terror grew palpable:

> The fear was so powerful that it seemed to make my personality completely evaporate. . . . "Whitley" ceased to exist. What was left was a body in a state of raw fear so great that it swept about me like a thick, suffocating curtain, turning paralysis into a condition that seemed close to death. I do not think that my ordinary humanity survived the transition to this little room. I died, and a wild animal appeared in my place.[6]

We now enter the fantastical world of abductees, who typically find themselves in strange-looking—and smelling—rooms that are a far cry from our expectation of an intergalactic spacecraft built by a vastly superior civilization. While details of each case vary, common features of the abduction experience show up again and again, namely the appearance of space beings known as the "greys."

Strieber recounts several variations, including small robotlike beings and those wearing dark blue coveralls. He describes them as having "deep-set eyes, pug noses, and broad, somewhat human mouths." Others bore little resemblance to anything human: "The most provocative of these was about five feet tall, very slender and delicate, with extremely prominent and mesmerizing black slanted eyes."[7]

If you are starting to get seriously freaked out, try to comprehend what was about to happen to Strieber. A long needle was produced, and he was informed telepathically that it would be inserted into his brain. With a *bang* and a flash, an unearthly "operation" was performed on his cranium.

> The next thing I knew I was being shown an enormous and extremely ugly object, gray and scaly, with a sort of network of wires on the end. It was at least a foot long, narrow, and triangular in structure. They inserted this into my rectum. It seemed to swarm into me as if it had a life of its own. Apparently its purpose was to take samples, possibly of fecal matter, but at the time I had the impression that I was being raped, and for the first time I felt anger.[8]

In *Communion*, Strieber attempts to buttress these unfathomable claims with polygraph tests and affidavits from psychiatrists. To his surprise—and chagrin—his sessions with Dr. Klein uncovered earlier abduction experiences.

In one transcript, Strieber describes an episode from the previous October. On that night, beings entered his bedroom and touched his head with something resembling a magic wand, causing visions of planet earth engulfed in flames to explode in his mind. Several weeks later the beings reappeared in his bedroom, and Strieber was spirited away. This time the beings appeared to be interested in his sexual responses, and after another intrusive operation, announced: "You are our chosen one."[9]

Communion was the choice of large numbers of readers, spending almost a year on the *New York Times* bestseller list. Strieber began receiving letters by the thousands, many of which described abduction experiences that were equally horrific. By this time, various researchers had begun compiling abduction accounts. Walt Andrus, founder of the Mutual UFO Network (MUFON), noted that Strieber's experience was "frankly mild" in comparison to numerous other published accounts that he had investigated over the past decades.[10]

In his sequel, *Transformation: The Breakthrough*, Strieber elaborates upon the fear he experienced, and identifies the entities by using biblical parlance:

> I felt an absolutely indescribable sense of menace. It was hell on earth to be there [in the presence of these entities], and yet I couldn't move, couldn't cry out, couldn't get away. . . . Whatever was there seemed so monstrously ugly, so filthy and dark and sinister. Of course they were demons. They had to be. And they were here and I couldn't get away.[11]

Just like those reputable citizens reporting Bigfoot encounters, Strieber has expressed no doubt about the reality of his experience. Further, he has discerned that the bizarre creatures he encountered came not from some lofty intergalactic civilization but from an evil realm of darkness.

For One's Own Good

What explanation did Strieber give for this gruesome encounter with what he described as demons in the night? He drew a conclusion that is different from what we might imagine. Incredibly, Strieber convinced himself that the horrors he experienced, including cruel and painful violations of his person, were actually blessings in disguise bestowed by loving entities for his spiritual progression:

> I was a partner in my experience, and possibly its master. Before the nine questions, the visitors seemed to be in total control. They were terrible, implacable predators. Now I knew a truth: I loved them, wanted them, needed them, chose them, and called them. I was responsible for the visitor experience becoming a part of my life. I was not being randomly oppressed by them. I saw us on our little blue planet hanging in the dark, and suddenly I felt loved and cherished by something huge and warm and incredibly terrible.[12]

It is not difficult to imagine self-deception in his assessment of the abuse—and more than a passing resemblance to the Stockholm Syndrome, an irrational psychological response in which victims bond emotionally with their abusers, to the point of defending and identifying with them.

In Strieber's case, the supposed benefits of his abuse are exceedingly difficult to quantify. In what possible way could the trauma of having a scaly triangular object forced up one's rectum by pitiless entities qualify as a loving contribution to one's spiritual enlightenment?

In *The Screwtape Letters*, C. S. Lewis's satirical exchange of letters between a senior and a junior demon, the ranking devil emphasizes the importance of making their presence known to earthlings, because "when the humans disbelieve in our existence we lose all the pleasing results of direct terrorism and we make no magicians." The Paranormal Conspiracy engages in just that spiritual terrorism through unearthly cryptids and alleged space aliens that spread chaos and fear. Ironically, while this infernal conspiracy denies the reality of absolute evil as well as the existence of irremediably evil beings, that negation opens the door to unspeakable machinations of the devil, such as experienced by Strieber and others on these pages.

These entities are said to present themselves interchangeably as either positive or negative influences, depending on what lessons their human subjects need to learn. Yet, in Strieber's case, there is no denying the hideous abuse inflicted upon him—not least of which was the grievous lie that it was all for "good." And as we shall see in a moment, despite the supposed gains of having "faced the fear" by viewing the brutality as a supremely loving act, when Strieber faced the crisis of a lifetime, his spiritual visitors were nowhere to be found.

As the years went by, the veil of deception began to lift from Strieber. Though sometimes inconsistent in his views, he attributed a darker and more sinister motive to the alien entities in this explanation written in 2003:

> I'm a realist and what is now real is that the only thing that appears to be left of the contact experience is the dark side. So that's what we have to face now. . . . There are beings here who are hostile to one another, and some who hate us with a passion so great that it would be considered psychotic if it

was displayed by a human being . . . something so profoundly evil that it is almost beyond imagination.[13]

As writer and commentator on the paranormal Jason Horsley notes, however, such inconsistency is to be expected:

> Strieber often seems to be oblivious to how his theories conflict, and even cancel each other out. Yet paradoxically, that lack of consistency might be seen as evidence for the veracity of his accounts, because if Strieber were undergoing initiation into an alien paradigm, we would expect it to confound all expectations.[14]

In the Presence of the Lord

Strieber continued writing books that touched on the subject of the paranormal, several of which revisited his earlier experiences. Then one day, Strieber's life changed dramatically once again when his wife, Anne, who had been his mainstay, was struck by illness. Anne had been unfazed by the skeptics who mocked her husband as the "alien abductee Whitley Strieber" and worse, "the rectal probe man." He writes:

> Out of loyalty to me and faith in me, Anne had embraced my quest to understand the experience that I had written about in *Communion*. The idea of abandoning me had never crossed her mind. Instead, she'd taken the whole journey with me.[15]

Strieber noticed that his wife had been feeling out of sorts lately, but attributed it to her diabetes. One evening, as they were returning home from visiting their son, Anne turned to him and said: "Whitley, I want you to know that I've had a wonderful marriage."[16] He brushed it off, chiding her for not speaking in the present tense.

Minutes later, upon arriving home, Anne collapsed in the bathroom and was rushed unconscious to the hospital. She was diagnosed with a brain aneurysm, one that few patients survive.

There was nothing a shattered, disconsolate Strieber could do but pass endless hours in the hallway outside the intensive care ward where his wife lay unrecognizable, wrapped with gauze and hooked to tubes and needles.

Like others in our excursion into the metaphysical quest for love and ultimate meaning, Strieber had long drifted from the worldview of his Christian upbringing. His bizarre experiences with otherworldly beings had cemented his agnosticism regarding the God of the Bible and the teachings of the Church. Yet the alternative, a universe coldly governed by the impersonal "Law of Karma"—while perhaps compelling on an intellectual level—was strangely unfulfilling when Strieber faced the abyss.

He slipped into the back row of the hospital chapel, where a mass was taking place. In a poignant passage we are there with him, the lapsed doubter who had nowhere else to turn:

> After [the mass] ended, the priest came over to me. Doubtless my distress was completely obvious. He said, "Would you like me to pray with you?" And there it was offering me support in my anguish, an institution I had abandoned to its failure, had denied, had scorned, and whose beliefs I rejected. The priest's kindness was so palpable, flowing from the man's nature and his long experience, and there was now no holding back the tears, I found myself bawling like a baby.[17]

Strieber was appalled at his embarrassing display of weakness in front of the other congregants, and managed to choke out an apology. The discerning priest sought to comfort him: "God doesn't care about our failures. I learned that a long time ago. God waits. His door is always open."

In a remarkable passage, a broken Strieber then bares his soul to the reader:

> And so it was that the great searcher, the advanced esotericist, the delving, cynical philosopher, found himself stripped of everything except his need, and drawn by these simple words to the insight that the heart, not the intellect, is the seat of faith; it's the heart, and the heart proceeds by a different logic . . . and in that moment [I] understood the true exaltation of Jesus' admonition, "Except ye be converted, and become as little children, you shall not enter the kingdom of heaven." . . . He said the Lord's Prayer with me, this priest who I never saw again and whose name I never knew, and during the prayer I accepted that the presence that seemed to draw near was God, who, despite the vastness of his realm—and indeed, his own improbability—had a few moments for me.[18]

To be sure, Strieber's writings continue to show internal conflict, sometimes endorsing the "enlightenment" that the entities visited upon him, at other times noting the deception. But in the end, one senses the stark divide between the love shown by the priest, which so moved Strieber in the hour of his deepest need, and the "love" of the cunning entities who inflicted terror in the night.

Strieber is not alone in being inconsistent at this juncture. Many who seek the true light of genuine love can also be fascinated by the allure of darkness. As he admits: "The brain is a very, very complex organ, and consciousness travels along many and forked paths in its electric labyrinth."[19] Is it possible that the hidden motivations of our hearts can affect the choices we make along that labyrinthine neural pathway, distorting our judgment and making us vulnerable to deception by powerful unseen forces?

The forces behind the Paranormal Conspiracy are proficient at sowing confusion—blurring the lines between light and darkness, fact and fiction. As we have seen with the Bigfoot phenomenon—and again with Whitley Strieber—it is often a case of "credible persons reporting incredible things."

Rather than the wholesale fabrication of stories by significant numbers of reliable witnesses, the evidence suggests that such phenomena involve counterfeit sensual perceptions—a demonic virtual reality.

Alien Baby Factories

In *Close Encounters of the Fourth Kind*,[20] C. D. B. Bryan recounts stories told by abductees who attended a five-day UFO conference sponsored by the Massachusetts Institute of Technology. Bryan's book was hailed as masterful investigation—the exploration into an enigmatic phenomenon by a seasoned journalist "with no ax to grind." Curiously, as we shall see, Bryan's analytical judgment fails him at a critical juncture.

Two of his interviewees, Carol and her friend Alice, both from Maryland, had similar experiences on lonely country roads. Carol's story of abduction began when she was on her way to visit her parents one overcast afternoon. Inexplicably, she exited the interstate, ending up on a rural gravel road where through the fog she saw a small figure ahead.

All at once she felt herself floating upward along with the being. Their destination? A large dark object above them in the sky that Carol described as "enormous, maybe one hundred feet across. And it felt solid." The next thing Carol knew she was lying prone in a sort of room. And she was not alone: The type of alien known as a "tall grey" was beside her. A tall grey is identified by a long face with pointed chin and oval eyes.

She would come to call this tall grey "Doctor Being" because of the "medical tests" she was forced to endure. The being held what looked like a double-barreled syringe in his hand.

"A needle came out of each cylinder," Carol told me. "And each cylinder was fed by a tube. There was some sort of yellow-gold liquid in the syringes and he injected it into me here on my thumb."

Carol holds her hand out to me. The faint mark of a double puncture wound is still visible in the meat of her right thumb.

"The holes are scarring up now," she says. "But he injected all of this yellow-gold fluid through those needles into my thumb and it hurt like hell!" . . . Carol felt "a fierce burning sensation" as the fluid was pushed in. Everything about the procedure hurt, and Carol remembers tears trickling down the bridge of her nose.[21]

Carol would suffer a great deal more at the hands of her abductors. But this episode, mercifully, was ending. The floor opened beneath her and Carol began to fall slowly down to the canopy of trees. She was dropped near her car and, profoundly shaken, climbed in and was able to make her way to her parents' home.

The memory of the abduction was suppressed from Carol's consciousness. The only hint of anything suspicious was spotted by her mother, who noticed the puncture wounds on her thumb. That and her parents' kitchen clock, which revealed that there was an hour and a half of missing time in Carol's afternoon.

Alice had a similar encounter with alien beings, ironically also after making an unexpected turn off the highway. She was on a business trip when she found herself on a country road. As she came to a stop sign she saw small gray beings ahead, signaling to her. Like Carol, Alice floated up with them into a craft suspended high above in the night sky.

The excruciating experience would later be revealed in a session with Hopkins where, under hypnosis, Alice began feeling severe pains in her lower abdominal area. Hopkins asked her to describe what was happening:

"I feel like I just had a baby!" Alice cries, her voice breaking.
"You feel like you just had a baby."
"I wasn't pregnant!" she sobs.
Hopkins probes for a description:
"It's tiny. It's very tiny," Alice says, with a hint of revulsion.
"How tiny is it?" Budd asks.
"About the size of a pear . . . Ohhhh!"[22]

As the newborn creature was taken away, Alice recalled: "They say it's theirs." Hopkins then regressed the still-hypnotized Alice back to another painful episode when she was artificially impregnated during another abduction.

More abductions would follow for Carol and Alice, more sessions with "Doctor Being," involving the injection of colored fluids into their bodies as they lay exposed and terrified in otherworldly craft. Bryan's narrative here accords with a theory held by many abduction researchers—namely, that aliens from other galaxies are coming to earth to create alien/ human hybrids that can then be used to repopulate their dying planets.

Promoters of this planet-repopulation motive, however, do not address the fact that the procedures used are generally a crude variation of earthly medical practice rather than the technology of a civilization advanced millions of years beyond our own.

Virtual Friends in Virtual Places

Separately under hypnosis, Carol and Alice told Hopkins the same bizarre abduction incident where they were escorted together by aliens into a cavernous underground hangar that housed a massive UFO craft. About a hundred people were milling about, many of whom Carol and Alice knew, but they do not concur regarding the friends and acquaintances that they saw. This troubled Hopkins, who was very much invested in demonstrating that abductions are actual nuts-and-bolts experiences taking place in time and space.

He pressed for details about identifiable people in the abductions who could be verified. Still under hypnosis, Alice affirmed that she had talked with a college friend named Tiffany whom she had not seen for many years. When Alice was asked specifically about the content of this conversation, she relayed two bits of information: Tiffany told her she had become a pediatrician and was now living in Sacramento, California.

And here the otherwise astute Bryan seems to miss the enormity of what transpires next. New information that he receives from Alice should have broken open his entire investigation, taking it in another direction entirely. But he let it pass by—just a few matter-of-fact sentences in parentheses:

> (Ten days after this session Alice is able to locate Tiffany and speak with her by telephone. Tiffany is living not in Sacramento but in Cleveland, and she is not a pediatrician, but an anesthesiologist. She has never lived in Sacramento, and never left Ohio during the period [the] dream took place.)[23]

Bryan moves on as if unaware of the implications of the parenthesized information. Yet the erroneous facts about Tiffany call the entire premise of the alien abductee conference— that these are real experiences in real physical places—into question. If Alice did not really talk with Tiffany, what other facts are called into question? We are left to wonder about the underground hangar with the UFO, and the other people, and all the grotesque experiments.

So was their alleged abduction by aliens in the underground cavern simply a figment of their imaginations? The correlation of many of the details that Carol and Alice related to Hopkins separately under hypnosis argues against such a conclusion. Rather, the evidence indicates that Carol and Alice were in the grip of a virtual reality engineered by entities in possession of suprahuman abilities, the magnitude of which exceeds our ability to grasp. Yet—as we have already seen—the phenomenon is maddeningly inconsistent, with some facts and details being verifiable and others clearly false. We will in due time offer suggestions as to why this is the case.

Even that icon of abduction research, Dr. John Mack, who co-chaired the M.I.T. conference, had a change of heart about what was going on with the alien abduction phenomenon. After spending the prime years of his career defending the reality of the experiences of abductees, he came to consider them as "visionary events" that—while "real"—were more transcendent than physical in nature.

While not denying the possibility that some abduction experiences could involve physical spacecraft, Mack nevertheless admits:

> I can see now that I had to a large extent created my problem with the literalness that I had treated the encounter phenomenon in the 1994 book. It is possible that in some cases people are taken bodily into spacecraft. However, the question is more subtle and complex.[24]

The problem, according to Mack, is the Western materialist paradigm, which demands scientifically repeatable evidence. He had come to embrace in an expanded notion of reality that is not limited to a three-dimensional universe, but extends far beyond to include spiritual phenomena. In other words, there is no reason to believe that Carol and Alice left their cars or other physical environments during the times of their abductions. Again, this does not mean that Carol and Alice made up their stories or imagined their experiences. Far from it. Their abductions were more profound and experiential than any dream state could produce.

Viewed in this light, the alien abduction accounts seem to support an "expanded notion of reality," which includes other planes of existence that, under certain limited conditions, intersect with our world. The stories of the abductees further indicate the existence of interdimensional intelligences that have the ability to manipulate our consciousness, forming a demonic virtual reality within the mind. But this subterfuge does not always accord with the facts, as in the experience of Carol and Alice in the underground hangar. Though it is clear that Alice did not speak with Tiffany, other similarities in their accounts point to an interdimensional choreographing of their mutual experience.

Intriguingly, the entities can on occasion leave physical traces, such as the puncture wounds on Carol's thumb after her abduction. Rather than constituting definitive proof, the fleeting nature of such evidence instead resembles tantalizing but insubstantial magic or deceptive trickery.

The baffling mingling of suggestive evidence and misinformation is a hallmark of the Paranormal Conspiracy, and supports the idea of demonic deception. In fact, one wonders if Bryan's glossing over the vital information regarding Tiffany, contrary to his usual penetrating analysis, is a typical consequence of immersion in this unfathomable matter. Does it lead to one's critical faculties being compromised? Was he succumbing to the same influence?

The Siren Call of Spirit Love

Another intriguing observation of the M.I.T. conference is the fact that most—perhaps all—of the abductees giving presentations had experienced multiple abductions; some described lifetimes of paranormal experiences. One outcome of the conference was the speculation that the abduction phenomenon is intergenerational, which would help explain peculiar happenings in Carol's family.

As a youth, her father had episodes of unexplained missing time. Even more bizarre was what happened to her grandfather. One day, when Carol's dad was still a young man, the family had gathered for a holiday meal. Suddenly Carol's grandfather pushed his chair away from the table and announced that he was going to buy a pack of cigarettes.

His family stared at him: Carol's grandfather did not smoke. Why would he get up from the dinner table to go buy cigarettes? Was he up to something? Perhaps a surprise of some kind? He got into his car and drove away—never to be seen again.

Carol's grandfather was a concert violinist and respected member of the community. His car was found parked at the grocery store in town, but no trace of him was ever found. Years later he was declared legally dead.

Those who knew him asked, "Why did he abandon his family?" Carol recalled that he was a devoted husband, but she also noted that there were times when her grandfather would act oddly. He would leave for a couple of hours and return "very upset, very tired."

Did an unearthly attraction seduce Carol's grandfather away from his family on that day long ago? It is possible. In the two stories that follow, told over the next four chapters, we see the extent to which individuals will go to answer the siren call of psychic forces. These are cases in which two men—one a world-famous explorer, the other a hardheaded journalist—are conquered by the world of ethereal spirits, and literally sacrifice their lives to the beings that entice them.

THE LOST CITY OF Z

You have to quit confusing a madness with a mission.

—Flannery O'Connor, *The Violent Bear It Away*

I t was an adventure story that captivated a generation heady with possibility. Just after the Great War, before the storm clouds of the Third Reich darkened the horizon, a celebrated adventurer vanished while on a mysterious quest for fabled lost cities in the Amazon jungle.

The "Lost Hero of the Roaring Twenties" was English explorer Percy Harrison Fawcett, born in Torquay, Devon, in 1867. The date of his death is unknown—indeed, those closest to Fawcett believed that the explorer survived long after he supposedly perished, daring to hope that the bizarre visions of alien civilizations whispered in his ear by discarnate spirits might somehow, after all, be true.

Fawcett came from a family of some standing: His father was a member of the Royal Geographic Society and was in service to the future Edward VII. He was also a womanizer and raging alcoholic who squandered the family fortune, drinking himself to an early grave at the age of 45. Fawcett's mother was distant and cruel. An unpublished family biography notes tactfully that she was "not disposed to remain faithful to her unfaithful husband."[1]

Determined to preserve their social ranking, Fawcett's parents managed to scrape together the money to ensure that he would receive a proper education in Britain's elite secondary schools, notorious for their harsh discipline. He excelled at sports and gained a reputation for his "almost maniacal determination" to prevail on the playing field. On one occasion he held his position during a rugby match despite just having had his two front teeth knocked out.

At age seventeen, Fawcett was sent to the Royal Military Academy, which introduced him to new heights of institution-sanctioned cruelty. Plebes were subjected to hours of drills and floggings for slight infractions. Two years later, Fawcett was graduated, well schooled in the supremacy of the English way of life and prepared to do his bit to ensure that the sun never set on the British Empire. He was assigned to the Royal Artillery and posted to Ceylon (modern Sri Lanka). He was later trained by the Royal Geographical Society in navigation, survival and anthropology, and took up surveying while working for the British Secret Service.

It was in Ceylon that Fawcett found two great loves to replace the parents whose affection he scarcely knew—and which charted the tragic course of his life. The first was a taste for adventure, nurtured as he investigated ancient ruins in the interior jungle of the island.

The second was a young lady in attendance at a ball held in honor of Archduke Franz Ferdinand, heir to the Austro-Hungarian throne. Fawcett managed to procure an introduction—Nina was the well-educated daughter of a colonial magistrate—and it was love at first sight. The next day he wrote home to tell his mother that he had met "the only one I want to marry." Two years later the rapturous couple was engaged, with the earnest Fawcett confessing: "My life would have no meaning without you."[2]

Enter Fawcett's scheming mother, who for unknown reasons disapproved of the match and "confided" to him that Nina had been unfaithful. It was the Victorian Age, which valued above all the twin virtues of chivalry and chastity. The accusation likely opened the old wound of his parents' mutual infidelity. Fawcett broke off the engagement immediately, telling her in a letter: "You are not the pure young girl I thought you to be." A heartbroken Nina returned to England to escape the scandal.

Years would pass before the lie was exposed. At long last, having learned of his mother's treachery, Fawcett wrote to Nina, begging her for another chance. She later confessed: "I thought I had no love left for him. I thought that he had killed the passion I had for him with his brutish behavior." But when they were finally reunited, the embers of love were quickly stoked: "We looked at each other and, invincibly this time, happiness jumped all over us. We had found each other again!"[3]

In January 1901 Percy and Nina were finally united in marriage. They settled into life in Ceylon. A son, Jack, who would play a key role in his father's mystical quest in South America, was born in 1903. Another son and daughter, Brian and Joan, completed the young couple's family. The children describe their mother as "bumptious"—opinionated and full of life, and nicknamed her "Cheeky" because "she always had to have the last word." It was just as well that Nina was strong-willed, as being a War Department wife in those days was not easy. With her husband away for much of the time, she raised the children and managed the household affairs on a pittance of a salary.

Behind the storybook façade of career and family, Fawcett was restless and discontented with the rigidity of Victorian society. When the opportunity arose to undertake an exciting new surveying project in South America, where the uncharted Amazonian rainforest beckoned, Fawcett did not hesitate. Vast interior regions of Brazil, including much of the million square miles of the Mato Grosso, remained to be explored. Between 1901 and 1921, Fawcett undertook seven major expeditions into the "Green Hell" of the Brazilian jungle.

Fawcett soon earned a reputation as the most intrepid— and ruthless—explorer of the Amazon. On one expedition, five members of his nine-man team starved to death; those on other treks suffered appalling injury and illness, or were driven insane. Several men were found unworthy and expelled from his expeditions or, aggrieved and bitter, deserted him.

Simon Bendle includes Fawcett in his list of "Great British Nutters":

Percy would spend weeks paddling doggedly up uncharted rivers in a leaky canoe, or trudging for days through tangled undergrowth or fetid, stinking swamps. Death stalked him: he saw companions drown and succumb to fever; some died of plain exhaustion; one bloke wandered off into the bush alone and wound up full of arrows. But always Percy pressed on, undaunted and unscathed, British to his bootstraps, apparently impervious to the suffering and fear around him.[4]

A former expedition member complained bitterly that Fawcett "would not stop to let us eat or sleep. We were working twenty-four hours a day and driven like bullocks before the lash." Fawcett dismissed such sentiments: "The strain has always been too much for members of my own parties. I have no mercy for incompetence."[5]

In 1916 the RGS awarded Fawcett the Founders Gold Medal for his achievements, and published his article "Bolivian Exploration" in its geographical journal. Fawcett's considerable gifts extended far beyond that of explorer and soldier. He was an artist whose works were displayed in London's Royal Academy, as well as a marine engineer who held a patent for a keel design that is used to the present day. Despite his achievements, Fawcett's military career faltered, and he never attained the coveted rank of full colonel. Never one to let technicalities stand in his way, he insisted on the title, and it stuck.

It seemed that Fawcett represented the Ideal Man of Victorian society—a man, however, with a fatal flaw.

Is That You, Boy?

The Great War affected the direction of Fawcett's life profoundly. Recalled to serve in the British Army, he fought in the Battle of the Somme, which in the first day claimed nearly twenty thousand men, with double that number wounded. Fawcett was awarded the prestigious Distinguished Service Order medal, scant consolation for the horrific images indelibly etched in his mind of comrades ripped apart by artillery and machine guns, or asphyxiated by a deadly fog of chlorine and mustard gas spreading inexorably across the battlefield.

During this tumultuous period, Fawcett's life intersected with that of the illustrious writer, Sir Arthur Conan Doyle of Sherlock Holmes fame. The elder Doyle was acquainted with Fawcett and reportedly drew on his experiences for his prescient 1912 novel *The Lost World*, about a group of explorers who disappear into the unknown jungles of South America.

Doyle had a long-standing fascination with mediums, and in 1916 stated publicly his belief in Spiritualism, a quasi-religious movement that promoted contact with departed spirits. Spiritualism was sweeping the English-speaking world, with millions of adherents in England and America.

Doyle's son Kingsley was one of the casualties struck down at the Somme. When Kingsley succumbed to his wounds, his bereaved father suddenly joined the "lost generation" whose lives were shattered by the untimely death of their loved ones. Doyle had, in fact, lost eleven members of his extended family in the war. Like so many who had lost faith in ordered, materialistic society, he turned to Spiritualism, which offered the perceived comfort of being able to speak with departed loved ones.

Doyle's new faith became a personal crusade after attending a séance in which he attempted to contact his deceased son. He was taken aback to hear a familiar voice speaking through the medium:

> I said, "Is that you, boy?"
> He said in a very intense whisper and a tone all his own, "Father!" and then after a pause, "Forgive me!"
> I said, "There was never anything to forgive. You were the best son a man ever had." A strong hand descended on my head which was slowly pressed forward, and I felt a kiss just above my brow.
> "Are you happy?" I cried.
> There was a pause and then very gently, "I am so happy."[6]

Ironically, Doyle's own Sherlock Holmes would have been aghast at his creator pursuing mediums, séances and Ouija boards. If he had assumed the mantle of his astute sleuth, he might have escaped the charges of gullibility that dogged him throughout his life.

In one glaring demonstration of credulity, Doyle awarded his *imprimatur* to a famous example of paranormal trickery known as the Cottingley Fairies. In 1917, photographs depicting two young cousins posing with elves in a Yorkshire garden caused a sensation. Doyle wrote articles and a book, *The Coming of the Fairies*, arguing passionately for their authenticity.

More sober examination revealed that the photographs were clearly faked: The fairies had the flat appearance of cutout figures—which, as it turned out, is exactly what they were. In later years the cousins admitted as much, with only a few die-hard Spiritualists continuing to believe that fairies pranced about a garden in Yorkshire. Doyle never recanted his belief in the Cottingley Fairies, despite the fact that the elves bore a striking resemblance to similar illustrations in a children's book in which he himself contributed a chapter. Many of Doyle's friends and colleagues considered his foray into the occult arts to be hopelessly misguided. Among the skeptics was his trans-Atlantic friend, the renowned magician and escape artist Harry Houdini. Doyle took Houdini on a tour of the best mediums in Europe in hopes of converting him to Spiritualism.

Initially Houdini was interested and expressed an earnest desire to contact his beloved mother. However, the master magician quickly became disenchanted after spotting the parlor tricks used by the mediums and soon embarked upon a crusade to expose fraudulent mediums. In his book *A Magician among the Spirits*, Houdini recounts his efforts to debunk psychics and mediums using his knowledge of stage magic and tricks. A cash prize was offered to any medium who could pass muster, but was never collected.

Many spiritualists believed that there was no earthly explanation for Houdini's impressive stage performances. Doyle was under the impression that Houdini was actually a powerful Spiritualist medium who used his paranormal abilities to accomplish his stunts, a charge that Houdini stoutly denied. Their friendship suffered a fatal blow after a séance in which Doyle's medium wife summoned the spirit of Houdini's Jewish mother, the wife of a rabbi, who reportedly greeted her son with the sign of the cross and a hearty "Merry Christmas."

Houdini continued to insist that he was open to the possibility of communication with the dead, but that he failed to find convincing proof. Before he died, he told his wife, Bess, that if it was at all possible he would contact her. They agreed upon a secret code, *Rosa belle believe!*, taken from a play in which Bess was performing when the couple met. Each Halloween for ten years after his death, Bess held séances hoping to hear the secret code, but without success. Once again we observe the age-old stratagem of playing upon the yearning for love and ultimate meaning for our lives, diverting that natural and God-given drive to a dark place of deception. The desperate longing for a dead son ended with Doyle becoming an object lesson for spiritual gullibility, and Houdini's devotion to his mother might have entrapped him but for the bungling antics of the spirits. As for Fawcett, his "spirit guides" wove a fantastic tapestry of a mystical lost city that proved impossible for the acclaimed explorer to resist.

Fawcett's Last Expedition

Long a student of ancient civilizations, Fawcett had become intrigued by stories about the ruins of cities deep in the jungles of South America and accounts of white Indians with blue eyes and red hair—the remnants of a lost race? He noticed architectural similarities in edifices constructed around the world and became convinced that all human societies arose from a single source now obscured by the mists of antiquity: the island alluded to in Plato's works as Atlantis.

The log of a doomed 1743 Portuguese gold-mining expedition fell into Fawcett's hands. It was the last report of the expedition, sent by Indian runner to the viceroy in Bahia, before it vanished. According to the log, the Portuguese explorers had stumbled upon ancient paved steps cut through a cliff wall, leading to a massive ruined city with wide streets, large buildings and temples. They copied down mysterious inscriptions that have never been deciphered. Gold glittered in a nearby river. Some fifty miles away the expedition stumbled upon ancient silver mines, abandoned except for two mysterious fair-skinned men who—so read the report—escaped into the jungle. Fawcett labeled the city "Z."

Back in England, Fawcett began putting together an expedition to find Z. Unable to afford a proper complement of men and equipment, he settled on two companions: his eldest son, Jack, who aspired to become a movie star in Hollywood, and Jack's boyhood friend Raleigh Rimmell, described by one chronicler as "a joker with an eye for the ladies." With this formidable retinue, Fawcett made his final preparations before sailing back to South America.

In our age of instant news, it is perhaps difficult to appreciate the pace of life in the 1920s. The Roaring Twenties were, to be sure, a time of social and artistic dynamism, of new discoveries transforming the landscape of human experience. It was the day of art deco, jazz and flappers, as well as radio, telephones and motion pictures, all made possible by Edison's magic wires. The name *Percy Harrison Fawcett* personified the search for new frontiers, and, with no war to occupy men's minds, sensational stories about the indomitable explorer topped the headlines in newspapers and serials coast to coast. "What is Fawcett going to do next?" was the topic of the day.

His search for the lost city of Z promised to be the culminating expedition of a remarkable career. Before he and his team departed, Fawcett penned curious instructions for those who would be awaiting word of his success—or failure: "I don't want rescue parties coming to look for us. It's too risky. If with all my experience we can't make it, there's not much hope for others. . . . The answer to the enigma of ancient South America—and perhaps of the prehistoric world—may be found when those old cities are located and opened up to scientific research. That the cities exist, I know."[7]

It would take half a century for the reason why Fawcett did not want to be followed to be revealed.

In April 1925, Fawcett's party struck out for the great uncharted wilderness between the Xingu and Araguaia Rivers, southeastern tributaries of the Amazon. Far in the distance, above the impenetrable jungle canopy, rose the Serra do Roncador ("Snoring Mountains"), where Fawcett hoped to find the lost city of Z. Several hard-fought weeks later, as the party sliced its way through undergrowth and crossed streams too many to count, their Indian guides refused to go on, instinctively fearing the savages in interior regions that lay beyond the remote hamlets and tracks.

This was of no consequence to Fawcett: He and his two companions would continue with minimal provisions. The guides were sent back with a message for his wife: "You need have no fear of failure."

Nina guarded this hope in her heart as the weeks and months passed. After two years even the most stalwart believers in Fawcett's invincibility had given up. But not Nina. For two decades she kept watch faithfully, awaiting news that never came.

The Hunt for Colonel Fawcett

In the years after Fawcett and his two companions disappeared, despite his express wishes, more than a dozen expeditions were launched to discover what happened to them. More than a hundred men perished in the hunt.

In 1928 his primary sponsor, the North America Newspaper Alliance, announced the formation of an expedition to join the search. Applications poured in from doctors, actors, prizefighters and steeplejacks—including one hopeful application sent from prison.

Commander George Dyott of the Royal Geographical Society was put in charge. In May 1928, he led a large, well-equipped party from Fawcett's old Dead Horse Camp into the Mato Grosso, striking out northeast to the Rio Kuluene. There the chief of the Anauqua Indians offered alarming information. Fawcett's party had reached the river sometime in 1925, but both the younger Fawcett and Rimmell were on the verge of collapse, and unable to speak. Wholly in character, a determined Fawcett was at that point literally dragging his charges along with him into the jungle.

The Anauqua told Dyott that they had tracked the campfires of the men. On the sixth night there was no fire, and they believed that Fawcett and his men had been slaughtered by the warlike Suya tribe. But as would happen so often in the case of the missing Colonel, there was a competing claim. When the party crossed the river to the neighboring Kalapalo Indians, Dyott was informed by their chief that the Anauqua were lying to cover the fact that they themselves had killed the explorers.

Their account in turn was soon put in doubt by another alarming piece of evidence: A nameplate from one of Fawcett's cases was discovered hanging around the neck of a Kalapalo tribesman. The party began to hear taunts that Fawcett's grave would be their own. In fear for their own lives, Dyott and his men managed to slip away under cover of darkness, leaving behind much of their equipment. The news was flashed around the world, but only served to stoke the imaginations of a new generation of adventurers, many of whom set out in search of Fawcett.

The years came and went, replete with reported sightings and legends about Fawcett's fate. A notary public in Cuiaba, the capital of Mato Grosso state, recorded no fewer than fifty depositions attesting to Fawcett's whereabouts. To be sure, many were utterly contradictory: everything from having viewed the Colonel's dried and shrunken head to seeing him happily married to four native women and worshiped as a god. Only two artifacts surfaced in all the years following Fawcett's disappearance: the plate bearing his name, and his surveying compass. It was considered unlikely that the indestructible Colonel had succumbed to illness or starved to death: The smart money was on treachery and murder.

In 1948 what appeared to be confirmation emerged when the chief of the Kalapalo Indians confessed to clubbing the white men to death after Jack Fawcett had impregnated a local girl. Several years later Fawcett's younger son, Brian, was invited to join a highly publicized expedition to the graves, cameras flashing while he reluctantly shook hands with "his father's killers" as the accompanying press prepared to break the story around the world.

The bones were exhumed and returned to England for proper burial. Before interment, however, they were examined by the Royal Anthropological Institute and found not to belong to the six-foot-two Fawcett, but to a much shorter Indian. Something else was amiss. Brian had brought along his father's spare set of dentures, which consisted of two front false teeth to replace those lost in the school rugby match. The unearthed skull sported a complete set of intact front teeth.

But why let a few facts spoil a sensational conclusion to the search for the most celebrated explorer of a century?[8] Time would tell that there was much more to the story of what lured Colonel Fawcett into the dark reaches of Amazonia in search of the mysterious Z.

THE GREAT SCHEME

Ever has it been that love knows not its own depth
until the hour of separation.

—Khalil Gibran

Years—and decades—have passed, and the fate of Colonel Percy Fawcett remains as much a mystery as when he chopped his way deep into the Amazonian jungle in 1925. Yet even more intriguing than his disappearance is the question of what drove him into perilous territory in search of the elusive Z. It seems that Fawcett, the intrepid explorer with his feet solidly on *terra firma*, was driven by the world of ethereal spirits.

The better part of a century after the Colonel's party disappeared, Czech writer/director and Fawcett researcher,

Misha Williams, managed to gain access to the Colonel's private papers—what he calls the "Secret Papers"—which were hidden from public view in the Cardiff, Wales, home of Fawcett's granddaughter, Rolette de Montet-Guerin.[1] The story of the Colonel and his family, as revealed by the Secret Papers, was worlds apart from the picture-book perception they carefully crafted. Williams writes: "Fawcett's real story has nothing to do with poisonous snakes, sweaty armpits and swinging machetes in mosquito jungle-hell. It is all about the mind, the emotions and an inner quest."[2]

To understand what lay hidden in the depths of Fawcett's psyche, the paranormal connections that goaded him into a bizarre gambit in Amazonia, we must return to his early days in Ceylon and a visit by his older brother, Edward, whom Fawcett idolized.

Edward was deeply involved in the Spiritualist movement and a devotee of Madame Helena Blavatsky (mentioned in chapter 4 as a significant influence on George Adamski).

By dint of her commanding personality and alleged extraordinary psychic abilities, Blavatsky would do more than any single individual of her age to promote Eastern religious, philosophical and occult concepts throughout the West. She continues to have an enduring following, and is rightfully called the first doyen of the New Age movement. In the words of one contemporary admirer:

> In place of religious beliefs that portrayed salvation as something granted once and for all by the arbitrary act of a judgmental god, Blavatsky described a spirituality in which souls evolved over countless incarnations, gradually growing in

wisdom and power through literally unimaginable cycles of time.[3]

By 1887 Blavatsky's *The Secret Doctrine*, destined to become the single most influential work on occultism in a century, was a disorganized three-foot-high stack of scribbled notes and papers. Marion Meade, in *Madame Blavatsky: The Woman behind the Myth*, writes that while sojourning in the Belgian seaside resort of Ostend, Blavatsky received a letter from

> one of the few remaining members of the London Theosophical Society, a journalist and subassistant editor of the *Daily Telegraph* named Edward Douglas Fawcett. . . . Fawcett was not yet twenty-two years old. He wondered if Madame needed editorial assistance on her book; if so, he would be happy to come over to Ostend and lend a hand.[4]

Like other Theosophists, Edward was drawn to the religions of the East, and after completing his work on *The Secret Doctrine* traveled to Ceylon for further instruction in Buddhism. Fawcett would later join his brother in converting formally to Buddhism. It was an unorthodox act for a military officer in nineteenth-century Britain, whose mission was to encourage the conversion of the heathen to the Christian way of life and culture, not the other way around. British novelist and historian A. N. Wilson noted in *The Victorians*: "At the very time in history when the white races were imposing Imperialism on Egypt and Asia, there is something gloriously subversive about those Westerners who succumbed to the Wisdom of the East, in however garbled or preposterous a form."[5]

Ironically, Edward, who introduced Fawcett to the ways of the East, eventually abandoned Theosophy, while his younger brother plowed headlong into increasingly dangerous metaphysical waters. Fawcett was intrigued by Blavatsky's vision of lost civilizations. He became convinced that the lost city of Z was an outpost of extraterrestrial gods who came to earth in deepest prehistory, one of the "first rock cities" the "Lemurians" built "out of stone and lava," according to Blavatsky.

The High Priestess of Isis

Who was this Russian mystic who, perhaps more than any other individual, was responsible for Percy Fawcett's ill-fated adventure in Amazonia? Marion Meade, one of Blavatsky's most dispassionate biographers, wrote that during her lifetime people across the globe debated furiously whether she was "a genius, a consummate fraud, or simply a lunatic. By that time, an excellent case could have been made for any of the three":

> Blavatsky was short and fat, with bulging eyes and folds of skin falling from her multiple chins. Her face was so broad that some people suspected she was a man. She professed to be a virgin (in fact, she had two husbands and an illegitimate son) and an apostle of asceticism (she smoked up to two hundred cigarettes a day and swore like a soldier). Meade wrote, "She weighed more than other people, ate more, smoked more, swore more, and visualized heaven and earth in terms that dwarfed any previous conception." The poet William Butler Yeats, who fell under her spell, described her as "the most human person alive."[6]

Helena Petrovna Blavatsky was born to nobility in a nineteenth-century Russia steeped in superstition. With a soldier father who left home in service to the tsar shortly after her birth in 1831, and a mother who also deserted her for long periods, one wonders how a profound sense of abandonment affected the course of Blavatsky's life. She would later insist that her mother died when she was yet an infant, prompting one commentator to observe that the false claim

> seems to suggest that there was strife between the mother and daughter. It indicates a conflict between the wills. . . . Helen resented her mother's long absences, her intimate friendships in the bohemian world of letters, and felt it as a desertion of the home and herself.[7]

Even at an early age Blavatsky evidently felt the dearth of familial love: She was often sick and given to emotional hysteria and convulsions. Her life was characterized by the defiance of the conventional mores, which had failed her so profoundly. She exhibited a peculiar interest in all things weird and fantastic—including the occult. According to local folklore, the "Old Russia" forests around her home were haunted by green-haired nymphs called *rusalkas*. In a macabre childhood incident, a four-year-old Blavatsky put a curse on a fourteen-year-old boy who taunted her, threatening to have the *rusalkas* tickle him to death. The startled boy fled from her presence. Fishermen would later pull his body from the river.

The young Blavatsky gained a reputation for having power over supernatural beings that were lurking just out of view and seeking to inflict harm upon the unsuspecting. The household servants carried her around the house like a living talisman, sprinkling holy water and chanting incantations as they went for protection against malevolent goblins. Blavatsky's behavior grew more outrageous as she reveled in her newfound faculties, throwing temper tantrums at attempts to restrain her. In desperation, her family arranged to have exorcisms performed on the young girl, to no avail.

Blavatsky's mother died when she was twelve, and, reportedly, foretold on her deathbed the troubled life that lay ahead for her troubled daughter: "Ah well, perhaps it is best that I am dying, so at least I shall be spared seeing what befalls Helena. Of one thing I am certain, her life will not be that of other women, and she will have much to suffer."[8]

Blavatsky was sent to live with her grandmother, a royal princess of the Dolgorukov family, who harbored a keen interest in the occult. The young Helena immersed herself in books on medieval occultism in her *babushka*'s library, which nurtured her conviction that she was the recipient of psychic abilities bestowed by unseen powers.

At this time Blavatsky began practicing automatic writing. A spirit calling itself "Mrs. T.L." began dictating in German, a language that Blavatsky had never studied. Blavatsky believed that Mrs. T.L. was not a deceased spirit but rather a woman living in Norway. She thus understood herself to be a medium not of the dead, but of advanced living beings, which became the basis for her lifelong mediumistic letter writing through which she claimed to channel the "Tibetan Brothers."

At the age of nineteen, escaping a sham marriage, Blavatsky fled from Russia and began an extended period of her life known as her vagabond years. Outside of her own often astonishing recollections, little is known with certainty about her life and travels in the intervening decades before she arrived in New York in 1873.

Blavatsky claimed to have traveled to the Middle East, then to Eastern Europe, where she was reunited with her father. They traveled together in Europe and London, where on her 21st birthday she was introduced to her Hindu teacher, who told her she would need three years' preparation in Tibet for the "important mission" that he had planned for her. Numerous and sundry travels followed, in Blavatsky's telling, to Central America and across the United States. In her autobiographical *From the Caves and Jungles of Hindustan*, Blavatsky relates several years spent living on the Indian subcontinent in the service of her spiritual teacher.

Further wanderings ensued, to Java, and again to the Middle East, Europe and Russia, before traveling to Tibet, where she claims to have spent several years at a Buddhist monastery. Considerable doubt has been raised as to whether Blavatsky was ever in Tibet.[9] Truth or fiction, the underpinnings of much of Blavatsky's life message were rooted in her esoteric connections to that magical land at the roof of the world. It was on the Tibetan plateau that she claimed to have mastered her psychic abilities, including levitation, clairvoyance, out-of-body projection, telepathy and materialization. Tibet was also where the exalted Masters, said to be in direct spiritual communication with Blavatsky, resided.

Blavatsky claimed that during her time in India and Tibet, she was thoroughly initiated into the "deeper mysteries" of Eastern philosophy. She rejected belief in the personal-yet-infinite God of the Judeo-Christian worldview in favor of "enlightenment," achieved when one succeeds in reuniting with the impersonal "Force" of the universe. In the monistic philosophy of the East, there is no God to offend and thus no sin—and no need of redemption. Only endless reincarnations as one strives to satisfy one's karma, or unalterable Law of the Universe, until at last one is free from all desire and from all vestiges of personality, merging into the endless, formless ocean that is nirvana. Blavatsky also continued to develop her psychic powers as a medium, and nurtured a growing reputation—or notoriety—for her alleged communication with spirits and ability to levitate objects.

But how much of her claims actually happened? Theosophist and Blavatsky scholar Geoffrey Barborka, in his not-unexpected favorable treatment of Blavatsky's travels, admits that little is actually known about the time between her failed marriage and her trip to America. The implication of this is not lost on Martin Brauen, Swiss anthropologist and specialist in Tibetology and Buddhism: "This is a period of over twenty years and, note well, the (crucial formative) period in which among other things Blavatsky is alleged to have been in Tibet!"[10]

Blavatsky was said to materialize "Mahatma letters" out of thin air, which were psychic communications from a brotherhood of reincarnated Tibetan mahatmas who were directing her to form a new religion. The resultant Theosophical Society taught that a spiritual hierarchy—the "Masters of the Ancient Wisdom," consisting of advanced spiritual beings—oversaw the cosmic evolution of all life. In a sop to Christianity, Theosophy listed Jesus among these "Ascended Masters" along with Buddha, Krishna and various other "Great Teachers."

Controversy swirled around Blavatsky, who took delight in defying traditional expectations at every turn, inspiring both devoted followers as well as former associates who accused her of fraud. Brauen offers an intriguing suggestion:

> Was she, as has repeatedly been claimed, a confidence trickster? Or was she convinced that others—in this case the Chohan Lama, one of the Mahatmas—were proclaiming their views and using her as a medium to do so? . . . HPB often lived in her own world, mysterious to those outside; had trouble distinguishing between reality and her own subjective perceptions; heard voices; felt she was the object of plots and conspiracies: in short, she had symptoms that are typical of schizophrenia.[11]

And then there was the problem of plagiarism. Blavatsky cited her sources as "lost texts" suspiciously available only to her or from her channeling of the Tibetan Brothers and other discarnate spirits. W. E. Coleman, a Spiritualist and contemporary of Blavatsky, in his thorough and devastating critique of her writings, concludes:

> There is not a single dogma or tenet in theosophy . . . in the teachings of Madame Blavatsky and the pretended adepts, the source of which cannot be pointed out in the world's literature. From first to last, their writings are dominated by a duplex plagiarism,—plagiarism in idea, and plagiarism in language.[12]

Professor of Buddhist and Tibetan Studies Donald Lopez said of those who uncritically accepted and promulgated Blavatsky's teachings: "First, they mystified Tibet, embellishing the realities of Tibet with their own mystical fancies, and, second, they mystified their readers, playing on the credulity of the reading public."[13]

The Great White Brotherhood

Fawcett's growing obsession with Blavatsky soon permeated the household. What emerges from the Secret Papers is the shocking story of a family immersed in occultism from its earliest days. The Fawcetts would host séances at their home, which Jack, Brian and Joan attended from an early age.

The Secret Papers also reveal that before Jack's birth Fawcett was visited by a delegation of Buddhist soothsayers, who informed him that he and Nina had been carefully selected to be the parents of a son who was the reincarnation of an "advanced spirit." The boy would be born on May 19, the traditional anniversary of Buddha's birth, and would possess identifying characteristics, including a mole on his right foot. Everything came to pass as predicted, reported Fawcett, and as the proud parents returned home with their newborn son, "crowds lined the route venerating the newborn evolved being."[14]

According to Williams, Jack was to be handed over to "Earth Guardians" called the "Great White Brotherhood," also known as the "Watchers" or the "Shining Ones," for what can only be described as possession: "His physical body was to be 'taken over' by one of the ancient brothers who would then be able to live even longer within Jack's healthy young physical frame."[15]

From his examination of the Secret Papers, Williams concludes that Fawcett and his enigmatic associate, New Zealander Harold Large, were in contact with perhaps hundreds of mediums who were invited to the Fawcett home for séances.

It appears that the discarnate spirits—the Earth Guardians, Watchers and Great White Brotherhood (the titles appear to be fungible, depending on which medium is in contact with which spirit)—directed Fawcett on everything from the route of his expedition to minutiae about supplies to take along.

Back in New Zealand, Large claimed to be in direct contact with the ethereal Council, whence he directed Fawcett as he planned his final expedition. There was a spiritual goal behind the publicly announced aim of discovering the ruins of a long-lost civilization: Fawcett intended to make contact with advanced spirit beings and found a colony of the chosen few in order to develop mystic consciousness. Once trained by the Brotherhood, Jack would eventually establish a similar colony in his birthplace of Ceylon. Fawcett's code name for this plan was "The Great Scheme."

We have now moved far afield from a search for the ruins of a city called Z to a "Great Scheme" involving the creation of a "super race" guided by "Divine Planners." In a 1923 article in the *Occult Review* entitled "Links with the Planetary Control," Fawcett laid out his bizarre views regarding the Watchers or "Great White Brotherhood, a class of spiritual beings who guide earth's destiny from mystical locations."[16]

It was imperative that the uninitiated not discover the actual purpose behind his final expedition lest they adulterate that which was intended for a select few. Based upon his examination of the Secret Papers, Williams comes to the astonishing conclusion that Fawcett, determined not to be followed, gave false coordinates for his route and was otherwise deliberately misleading regarding the true destination and motivation for his last expedition. Fawcett's true objective was not the impenetrable jungle of the Mato Grosso, but something far different, described by him as a desert, as well as ice-capped mountain country.

One immediately wonders how Fawcett came to mention deserts and mountain tunnels. With an elevation of only two to three thousand feet, there are no peaks in the whole of the Mato Grosso. And it has an average annual rainfall of fifty to sixty inches. The private correspondence of Brian in the Secret Papers provides a clue: "Daddy's pictured objective was constructed upon personal imagination, romantic notion and psychic confirmation by self-styled 'seers.'"[17]

The Mysterious "M"

Brian was one person who knew more than he was saying. In fact, Fawcett's "despised and overlooked" second son would play a major role in bringing a sanitized version of his father's story to the world's attention. His motivations were complex, with troubling currents stirring beneath the surface.

Brian grew up in his older brother's shadow, deeply resentful of Jack's exalted status as a reincarnated Anointed One. As one relative recalled: "Fawcett wrote and illustrated stories for Jack, depicting him as a young adventurer, and when Fawcett was home the two did everything together—hiking, playing cricket, sailing. Jack was 'the real apple of his eye.'"[18]

But Brian would show them all. Whereas Jack basked in his father's attention and sought to emulate his austere bearing, Brian excelled in the mystical arts. It appears that, for much of his life, he was under the influence of a "female earth spirit" that he referred to as "M." It was as a young child, when the family lived in Ireland, that he was first contacted by M. Brian considered himself more "spiritually evolved" than Jack—and even his father.

The Secret Papers suggest that M was much more than a discarnate spirit advisor to Brian. The portrait he painted of M in 1937 reveals a young woman with Celtic features, black hair and sparkling blue eyes. As the decades passed, his attachment held firm, as shown by the matured yet still vibrant matron of later portraiture in 1971. Brian's diary reveals a bizarre trans-dimensional relationship in which M is portrayed as residing in his home, which she used as a base while going off periodically to meet with other spirits.

This is not the only case of bizarre "spirit love" that we shall encounter, and here also in Brian's case, his discarnate "soulmate" was ever scheming to extend her control over his life. Brian's diary records his happy submission, convinced that when it came to matters of the spirit, he was more than equal to archrival Jack: "Each year becomes more important to me and 'M' bears me along with growing impetus and herself becomes more influential in my everyday normal activities."[19]

The Secret Papers leave little doubt that Brian concealed his father's spiritual quest deliberately, convinced that the world was "not ready" to be told the Colonel's true objectives. He published his own account, *Expedition Fawcett*,[20] which alleged that his father headed northeast from the regional capital Cuiaba, sending a continuous trail of Fawcett seekers off into the dense Amazon jungle, some of whom never returned. An entry in Brian's diary reveals what was behind this deliberate attempt to deceive:

This morning "M" said "You did a splendid job with *Exploration Fawcett*. You gave out the superficial story of your father which was just right for the masses. . . . What I don't want is a revelation of his mystic side."[21]

The acorn does not fall far—the saying goes—and Brian doubtlessly learned much about consultations with spirits from his father. Fawcett's daughter, Joan, showed Williams files crammed with letters to her father from mediums. Williams notes that what had long been concealed in the Secret Papers "is far more extraordinary than any of the wild theories that can be read on the Internet or can possibly be invented in a fictionalized dramatization."[22]

It now becomes clear why Brian, under the sway of M, concealed his father's true objective: The *hoi polloi* must be kept from stumbling upon and polluting the pristine ambience created by the enlightened few. In a letter to his son, Colonel Fawcett wrote of the city he sought:

I expect the ruins to be monolithic in character, more ancient than the oldest Egyptian discoveries. Judging by inscriptions found in many parts of Brazil, the inhabitants used an alphabetical writing allied to many ancient European and Asian scripts. There are rumors, too, of a strange source of light in the buildings, a phenomenon that filled with terror the Indians who claimed to have seen it. The central place I call "Z"—our main objective—is in a valley surmounted by lofty mountains. The valley is about ten miles wide, and the city is on an eminence in the middle of it, approached by a barreled roadway of stone. The houses are low and windowless, and there is a pyramidal temple. The inhabitants of the place are fairly numerous, they keep domestic animals, and they have well-developed mines in the surrounding hills. Not far away is a second town, but the people living in it are of an inferior order to those of "Z." Farther to the south is another large city, half buried and completely destroyed.[23]

Pondering this fantastical description, Brian mused about how much was based upon sound research and how much was based "on the babblings of clairvoyants."[24] Confident of his own spiritual advancement, how many times he must have pondered as the decades passed, "If only Daddy could see!"

Eventually, however, his bond with M would strain and break. His spirit paramour abandoned him, presumably for younger flesh. Brian was set tragically adrift. Sister Joan believed that M might have been responsible for his death.

Williams acknowledged that, while agnostic with regard to the supernatural: "I have to say that I have concluded through evidence that 'M' does have an objective reality and should be treated as a personality totally independent of Brian's subjective consciousness."[25]

The End of the Story

The Secret Papers reveal Fawcett's plan to have Nina and select others join him once the work of establishing the secret colony was well underway. In letters brimming with hope and expectation, Nina sought to rally the inner circle. In November of 1926 she wrote to one Major Mein:

> I think that before long we may call upon you—my husband and I—to help us in developing the new-found country, then, all the best types of men available will be wanted! . . . I hope before very long you may meet in person "The Fawcett Family."[26]

The months—and years—passed with no word of the Colonel. For her part, Nina kept the faith long after her husband disappeared. With an empty nest after the marriage of her daughter in 1928, she continued waiting alone for word from Amazonia. Large kept contact with her until 1936, encouraging her—doubtlessly egged on by his spirit contacts—that Fawcett and Jack were still alive, perhaps held captive by some remote tribe. There was talk of mounting a rescue mission. Mediums claimed to be in contact with Fawcett into the 1940s. Large and his spirit cohort eventually faded from the scene.

The years were not good to "Cheeky." She was shuttled between Brian in Peru, ever resentful for having to play second fiddle to Jack, and Joan in Switzerland. All Nina's worst traits were magnified as she became increasingly insufferable. Finally, impoverished and friendless, she met her end in a boardinghouse in austere post-war Brighton, England. One wonders what her thoughts were, as the years passed, of her beloved Fawcett and the great spiritual quest they shared, which was never to be.

Williams notes: "Nina was Fawcett's most loyal supporter and one could say her life was sacrificed to him and his memory."[27]

One piece of evidence that was ignored—or suppressed—by the inner circle, sheds light on his sad end. Four years after his disappearance, the Swiss trapper Stephan Rattin offered a very different story of the Colonel's whereabouts.

Rattin and two companions were traveling along the Arinos River in northwest Mato Grosso—not the northeast, the direction where Brian and others had insisted Fawcett had gone—when they came across a tall, elderly white man with a long beard who was being held captive by an unknown tribe of Indians. While his captors occupied themselves with draining Rattin's gifted bottles of liquor, the two had a chance to talk. The man said he was an English colonel, and showed Rattin a snake-eyed signet ring. He asked Rattin to contact his friend, a Major Paget in Sao Paolo, and inform him of his whereabouts.

Rattin would subsequently learn that Paget not only knew Fawcett, but had helped fund his last expedition. The man also asked him to contact the British Embassy and describe the ring to those who knew him. He did so, with mixed results. But Nina, whose hope burned eternal, confirmed that the description matched her husband's ring, setting the stage for a follow-up expedition.

There was one more piece of nigh indisputable evidence: The elderly man in the jungle also showed Rattin his dental plate, complete with two false teeth. In *Exploration Fawcett*, under compulsion by M to mislead the public about his father, Brian discounted Rattin's account. But in his diary—part of the Secret Papers—Brian admits: "I come to the conclusion that Rattin was telling the truth"[28]

In the meantime, Rattin announced that he would return to the jungle with his two friends and bring back the captive Colonel. Neither he nor his companions were ever seen again.

Before he disappeared into the jungle, however, Rattin relayed one last cry of despair from the elderly man in the jungle. He wished his loved ones to know that he was alive, but—here the old man broke down—his son was "asleep."

Alleged sightings of Fawcett continued for decades. There was, however, one sighting near Diamantino, northwest of Cuiaba, the direction revealed in the Secret Papers as Fawcett's true destination. A French engineer named Roger Courteville reported seeing an elderly English officer suffering from fever and delusion sitting by the side of the road:

> His heroic stoicism was so odd that I thought he must be a foreigner and addressed him at random in English—"I say, man, the mosquitoes seem to take care of you. . . ." My remark produced its effect and he looked up at me. His face showed obvious signs of fatigue and general weakness consequent on fever, but his eyes were straight and forceful, and I had the impression that this man had been a soldier. . . . Finally he replied: "Those poor animals are hungry too." We went on our way leaving the poor man calmly watching the mosquitoes devouring his legs.[29]

Under the sway of his spirit love, M, Brian was publicly skeptical, while admitting privately: "That sounds exactly like Daddy."[30] We will perhaps never know if it was Fawcett by the side of the road that day, a shell of his former self, shattered in body and soul by the loss of his hopes and dreams. And we will surely never know how often he thought of his beloved Nina in those last days, the one without whom, he once said, life had no meaning.

We are, however, provided a glimpse by Grann, who like Misha Williams had the opportunity to examine the Secret Papers in the living room of Fawcett's granddaughter. He recorded the two poignant lines of a poem inscribed on the inside cover of one of Fawcett's diaries, to give strength when all hope had fled in the godforsaken wilds of Amazonia:

> Oh love, my love! Have all your will—
> I am yours to the end

The Great Scheme, with Jack as the reincarnated Chosen One destined to become the embodiment of the exalted spirits, lay in ruins. The impenetrable jungle forever separated the weakened, aged explorer from family and home. Misled deep into a jungle trap, beguiled by deceitful spirits, was Fawcett the not-quite-full Colonel.

8

SPIRIT LOVE

Down, down, I sank, till immersed in that mighty
ocean where conflicting elements were swallowed
by a mountain wave of darkness, which grasped me
within its mighty folds and I sank to the lowest depths
of forgetfulness.

—Andrew Jackson Davis

Joe Fisher was a bright and likeable young Canadian journalist with a winning smile that charmed the ladies. Nonetheless, like so many of us, the veteran writer struggled to
find that enduring bond, the rapturous union of two souls.
What he chanced upon—or thought he encountered—was so
much more than that: an otherworldly passion that stretched

across the ages. He could scarcely believe his good fortune, and, in the end, his luck would run out.

Born and educated in England, Fisher immigrated to Canada, where he forged a reputation as one of the country's leading investigative reporters. He also had a lifelong interest in metaphysical topics and wrote several books on past-life experiences. His 1985 *The Case for Reincarnation* boasted a preface by the Dalai Lama, an impressive tribute to Fisher's stature as a writer.[1]

Fisher had long abandoned the Christian fundamentalism of his upbringing; his books were steeped in Eastern mysticism and taught that reincarnation is the prism through which all of reality is viewed. Though the concept of past lives is not found in the Bible, Fisher claimed that reincarnation was a primordial belief of early Christians and was suppressed by the institutionalized church. In his view, the Gnostics were the authentic Christians, while Rome and the fathers of the Church were guilty of censuring and eventually extinguishing the grand truth of the transmigration of souls. This line of argument was by no means original to Fisher; it is common to apologists of Eastern religions.

The Case for Reincarnation struck a chord, and Fisher was in demand on the media circuit. It was during an interview on a Toronto radio station that events were set in motion that would shake his Eastern worldview to the core. In his own words:

> Little did I know that I had embarked on a voyage that would turn my perceptions inside out and bring me to the brink of emotional collapse. Ambling in where angels fear to tread, I was well and truly embroiled in mediumistic phenomena

before the realization dawned that my rugged experience as an investigator was about as useful as a swimsuit on the moon.[2]

On the other end of the broadcast, a woman identified only as "Aviva"—a pseudonym, as with the other characters in this unfolding tragedy—was sitting by the radio in her apartment, listening intently. She wrote a letter that was forwarded to Fisher by his publisher. It was a cry for help, and unfolded a story almost too strange to believe.

Into the Mystic

Aviva worked as a laboratory technician, and was nothing if not utterly pedestrian in her life and belief system. Like many, she scoffed at the idea of psychic phenomena. Aviva was suffering from chronic myelocytic leukemia, a life-threatening disease which, as it turns out, was the least of her problems.

A neighbor named Roger was a hypnotist and offered to hypnotize her in order—he claimed—to administer healing suggestions to her subconscious mind. Despite her total ignorance of hypnosis, Aviva succumbed to the susceptibility of those in dire straits.

The hypnotic sessions seemed to help: After a few months the pain and nausea appeared to subside, as well as the inflammation in her deteriorating joints. The improvement, of course, could well have been due to her continuing to undergo chemotherapy and take traditional medicine. Like much of what would transpire, "proof" of the benefit of the hypnotism was never quite evident and maddeningly intermingled with doubt and confusion.

Still, on the whole Aviva felt it was worthwhile to continue with the hypnosis. Now indebted to Roger, Aviva felt obligated to agree to his suggestion that they attempt to communicate with what he termed "the guides" during their sessions. For her part, Aviva did not believe in or have any interest in speaking with any supposed spirits, but soon found herself channeling various "entities" and deeply involved in the psychic world.

After hearing Fisher on the radio, she reached out in hopes he could explain what was happening to her. Fisher, on the other hand, saw Aviva as an opportunity to prove reincarnation, using the convincing case of a skeptical middle-aged mother of three who was giving voice to disembodied spirits who described their former lives.

Fisher agreed readily to Aviva's invitation to make contact with these otherworldly entities. On July 20, 1984, he showed up at her Toronto townhouse and waited as she stretched out on the small sofa, shifting around to get comfortable. He was already envisioning a book about "discarnate beings," in which Aviva's case would be the crowning proof— an unanswerable firsthand case history—of the truth of reincarnation.

Reunited Love

Roger, sitting nearby and speaking in a somber monotone, began directing Aviva into a hypnotic state as she reclined motionless. Despite researching the subject of otherworldly spirits, Fisher had never actually attended a séance. It seemed to be taking a long time. He was starting to get distracted.

Suddenly Aviva's lips parted and she began to speak. Immediately Fisher's eyes were riveted on her supine form.

Aviva spoke, but the words belonged to someone—or something—else. The voice was that of a male speaking in a distinctive English accent who claimed to be Aviva's guide—the spirit of a man who had lived as a sheep farmer in Yorkshire during the last century. The guide—named "Russell"—had a special message for Fisher: He was ready to divulge the identity of Fisher's own guide, who was directly responsible for Fisher's welfare while he was on the "earthly plane."

Fisher listened dumbfounded as Russell—speaking through Aviva—revealed that Fisher's spirit guide was a woman named "Filipa." She claimed to have been with him, her charge, throughout many lifetimes, most recently in Greece between 1718 and 1771.

The hook was in. With consummate skill that easily overpowered Fisher's mortal defenses, the as-yet-unknown quantity calling itself Russell began to reel in its catch. Russell seemed to know precisely the chink in Fisher's armor and made a masterful appeal to his heartstrings—an appeal that would shortcircuit the doubts and incongruities Fisher's rational mind would be screaming during the long evenings to come in Aviva's cramped parlor.

And what an exquisite bewitching—an otherworldly love promised to transcend temporal earthly existence, a love so strong and terrible that it was compelled to manifest itself time after time. It was the yin-yang of two great souls embracing eye to eye and heart to heart in a cosmic dance throughout the ages.

At once nothing mattered for Fisher except to meet this Filipa, and to discover—or rediscover—that elusive love he had been searching for his entire life. But Russell was not about to grant access so quickly to what he had dangled so tantalizingly in front of his subject. Filipa was not ready, he explained, to speak herself: She would first have to "learn the energies" of the human vehicle (Aviva). In the meantime, Russell offered himself as an intermediator.

Fisher asked about his last relationship with Filipa, and was intrigued to learn that he was her suitor in the Greek village where they both had lived. He was told that he had committed a transgression and was sent from the village, never to return. The name of the village, according to Russell, was "Theros"—a crucial detail that would figure prominently in Fisher's later investigations.

By the time Roger interjected himself to bring Aviva out of her trance state, Fisher was under a potent spell of his own: "Such was my enchantment that . . . I was visualizing secret liaisons with a raven-haired beauty." From that moment he sought to be reunited with his timeless love, next to which all transient human affections paled in comparison.

The months passed. Fisher attended the Friday evening séances at Aviva's Toronto townhouse, increasingly obsessed with the woman he had loved and lost more than two centuries before. Among those troubled by Fisher's new obsession was his live-in girlfriend, Rachel. He persuaded her to attend, but she sensed a creepy negativity in the séances and eventually refused to go back. As his obsession with his ethereal paramour grew, Fisher was increasingly alienated from Rachel. But it mattered little compared to the promise of the love just out of reach: "Filipa gave the impression that, could she only have materialized, she would snuggle romantically beside me. Her messages . . . hinted at tenderness, seduction, shared confidence."

Fisher listened entranced as Filipa—still communicating through Russell—painted a romantic picture of their former life together in Theros. Filipa related how she had worked in the fields near the village, while Fisher had led a guerilla unit against the occupying Turks. If Fisher could only hear the Greek folk music that he used to sing lustily as he sat in the village plaza with his friends, claimed Filipa, it would surely rekindle long-lost memories of his former homeland.

And here we find the first inkling that all was not as it appeared. There would be many more. Intrigued by this snapshot of eighteenth-century village life in Greece, Fisher searched music stores in Toronto for recordings of old Greek folk songs played on traditional instruments. He finally obtained a recording, but was disappointed to be unmoved by the music. Any incipient doubts, however, would soon be swept aside by the first direct communication with Filipa.

It happened without warning: Suddenly Filipa came through in her own voice, "her Greek inflection lending charm to broken English. Her delivery was subdued, pensive and poignantly tender." To Fisher, Filipa always spoke to him "like a lover for whom the fire still smoldered." They enjoyed an easy familiarity forged through a long shared history. Joe was told that he had incarnated 2,045 lives over the past 21,000 years—seventeen of which he had shared with Filipa. Theirs was a bond that kept drawing them together time after time: "We will be earthbound again together," she promised.

Love Is All There Is

As Fisher basked in the warm glow of passion beyond compare, Filipa and the other guides waxed eloquently about the centrality of love. They claimed to exist in a realm beyond space and time that abounded in brotherly "mind-to-mind communication." Freed of material cares, the entities there sought to cultivate the one indispensable attribute: unconditional love. Fisher observed that "it seemed our allies in the next dimension were able to avail themselves of love and knowledge as easily as we received the blessing of sunshine."

Fisher was assured that there was nothing to fear about death. Russell explained that when one enters the spiritual dimension, "you will feel the love that your guide is bringing to you. . . . Here the feelings of love are far stronger, the ties with others and the feelings that go with those feelings are far deeper than on the earthbound plane."

Fisher was increasingly preoccupied with a more earthly expression of love:

> Filipa rapidly became an advisor, a best friend. And my ideal lover. Sometimes I fantasized about our sex life in eighteenth-century Greece and imagined with relish the passion that would erupt if only we could come together again, sharing hungry bodies as well as hungry minds.

His unearthly paramour expressed her deep affection for him, promising that one day they would be reunited on the spiritual plane, where they could resume their loving relationship.

Not surprisingly, Fisher's relationship with Rachel deteriorated as he was increasingly consumed by his infatuation with Filipa. His new obsession also cost him a number of old friends, one of whom noted sadly, "We've lost Joe."

Incredible Myths

During the Friday night séances, the spirit guides, led by Russell, were fond of discoursing *ad nauseam* on metaphysical topics, presented with a studied, sophisticated air. The genteel veneer gave way to cold sarcasm, however, when the subject of religion came up. Russell would launch into monologues criticizing the living for desiring "the security of a deity."

To his surprise, Fisher discovered that the divine being who was the object of Russell's contempt was none other than Jesus Christ, about whom Russell made astounding—and thoroughly heterodox—claims. Fisher had long "moved on" from Christianity, yet he was taken aback by Russell's contemptuous assertions about Jesus Christ. According to Russell, Jesus was "just a man" who, far from being the sinless Son of God, had found it necessary to undergo innumerable reincarnations to resolve personal karma.

As the others in the group sat quiescent, this was too much even for the backslider Fisher to swallow. He suggested that Jesus had achieved an impressive list of accomplishments, to which Russell retorted dismissively: "No, he didn't. He managed to get people to follow him . . . his life has been quite distorted. The fantasy has hung on long after the man has gone, and it has been blown bigger and bigger with each generation."

Fisher took another tack, asking Russell about another world religious leader:

"What about Buddha?" I inquired. "Has he reincarnated, do you know?"

"Buddha has a different aspect, altogether. The one who you call the Buddha has not reincarnated to my knowledge."

Thus, Buddha—having a "different aspect altogether"—apparently had no need of further reincarnating, unlike Jesus Christ, who as Russell claimed, still had "lots to learn":

"So, what sort of status would Jesus Christ have today? . . . Does he still have lots to learn?"

"Oh, the same as yourself," [Russell said]. "If you were living in desperate times and you spoke out with your books you, too, might be revered."

Russell continued, insisting that Jesus was "no more than a mere man," asserting that the teachings and beliefs about Him were "distorted fables": "Fables will be written around his life and they will be distorted into what you call scriptures."

On another occasion, Roger inquired about the resurrection of the body followed by the Judgment. Russell appeared shocked to learn of the belief, even though, as noted by Fisher, it was commonly held in Victorian society where Russell was allegedly incarnated. He found it incredible that such "myths" could persist in modern society, and assured the group that those holding to such beliefs would "learn" the truth once they reached the spiritual plane.

At the same time, Eastern mysticism was promoted uncritically in the discourses of the guides. Fisher summarized the teaching of the guides concerning the transmigration of souls and the ultimate goal of humanity in terms that mirrored the

Hindu concepts of nirvana or moksha: "By means of successive incarnations and subsequent progression through the non-physical planes, we were making our way back to that pure state of being where individuality would be freely and willingly surrendered." The expanding group that met at Aviva's townhouse, convinced that they were members of a fortunate elite, accepted such teachings uncritically. After all, only one in ten thousand—they were informed—could achieve contact with spirit guides and thus benefit from the wisdom of the ages.

Yet there were discordant signs. For one thing, Fisher was bothered by the guides' insistence that they honored the free will of their charges. Fisher found this to be dissembling in the extreme: The entities were nothing if not increasingly asserting their influence over the lives of those attending the Friday night séances, though he would not yet call it manipulation. Filipa, as always, could be counted on to lend a sympathetic ear to Fisher's concerns, gently compelling him not to let his questions overshadow the great truths he was learning.

Quest for Incontrovertible Evidence

As Fisher's stature in the realm of contact with otherworldly spirits grew, so did attacks of the skeptics. A turning point came when he appeared on the Canadian Broadcasting Company *Crossfire* program and faced withering criticism of his defense of reincarnation.

Investigator Doug Williams noted: "Joe's chosen path had led him here, to humiliation while pleading his case to professional cynics on the CBC."[3] Fisher's friend Kelly Watt remembers Fisher telling her after the *Crossfire* program:

"I'm going to have to defend this; I'm going to have to see the research through."[4]

The investigative journalist within Joe Fisher finally kicked in. He determined to prove the truth of reincarnation by uncovering evidence of the lives of the spirit guides who had allegedly incarnated in relatively recent times. Several of the more than twenty spirit guides that communicated through Aviva claimed to have incarnated in the twentieth century.

Fisher chose "William Alfred Scott," who claimed to be an Englishman and World War II bomber pilot with the Royal Air Force, as offering the best chance at validation. Accordingly, Scott, who went by the name "Earnest," was questioned carefully about his life in wartime England. Fisher noted that it was an impressive performance, with Earnest answering all questions forthrightly and convincingly.

Some details, however, caught his attention. Earnest had an odd tendency of lapsing into American pronounciations of certain British places—a peculiarity that no bona fide Englishman would be guilty of. Mostly, though, Earnest gave such a charming performance that, to Fisher, the discrepencies hardly mattered.

Armed with detailed notes and recordings of the sessions with Earnest, Joe Fisher flew to England in February 1986. After spending a few days with his mother, he made his way to the Public Record Office, where he spent several hours in the reading room, scanning logbooks for notations regarding Earnest's squadron.

Though a number of details checked out, one key piece of evidence eluded him: confirmation of one Flying Officer William Alfred Scott. It was not to be, to Fisher's inexpressible consternation. At the end of the day he left the building empty-handed: There was no record of Flying Officer Scott in any of the operations logbooks during the three years he claimed to have served.

Earnest be damned. The true test—the final, definitive proof for Fisher of the guides' past lives and reincarnations— lay with Filipa. Accordingly, he planned an ambitious investigative "pilgrimage to the past" that would put to rest his growing doubts and confusion.

Lost to the World

Fisher had already begun to withdraw from "ordinary existence," which was dreary and mundane compared to the inexpressible thrill of otherworldly communication with the guides: "My terrestrial life was doomed. No woman of flesh and blood could hope to emulate Filipa's love and concern."

He planned a trip to Greece and the village where he and Filipa had lived. On his way he would stop in England to seek confirmation of the past life of Russell, the group's primary guide and dominating force. Russell had mediated the controversy with Earnest and had himself issued warnings about the need to establish the authenticity of the claims made by any spirit. Fisher looked forward to his journey, well-prepared with many details of Russell's past life, and was confident of success.

The following summer Fisher was back in London poring through genealogical records from the late nineteenth century, the time when Russell said he had lived as a sheep farmer in a village called Heatherfield in Yorkshire. Surely after the debacle with Earnest and Russell's own sympathetic assurances, this venture would yield positive results.

But, alas, once again the public records were at variance with the claims of the discarnate spirits. Wondering if it could all be a "colossal oversight" on his part, Fisher drove north to Yorkshire, where he examined a magnificently detailed Ordnance Survey Map drawn in 1850, which included every "field, trough, well and shed" in the area.

But not Russell's farmhouse. As before, there was a confounding mixture of isolated details that checked out, while the main thrust of the guide's story could only be described as a cunning artifice. Fisher consulted local historians, who confirmed one or two of the family names mentioned by Russell, but others—including his own namesake—were unknown, and there was no record of his home village of Heatherfield.

In yet another maddening twist, it turned out that there *was* a St. Mary's Church, where Russell said he had been buried. Fisher was dismayed to learn, however, that the parish church had fallen into disrepair and was closed decades before Russell's death.

Stubbornly refusing to concede defeat, he wandered through the Yorkshire dales in search of a village that might fit Russell's story. As the day wore on, Fisher could no longer deny that the bucolic countryside belied a troubling reality. He was forced to face the "unassailable conviction" that the lives Earnest and Russell had claimed to live were little more than an intricate pretense. His sense of betrayal was palpable.

All was nearly lost—but not quite. The others were peripheral: Only Filipa had forged a bond with his innermost being, reaching out from the Hellenic world of old. Fisher now turned his sights on Greece: Surely his one last great hope would succeed, where the ethereal charlatans had failed, in establishing the ageless truth of reincarnation.

THEATER OF THE GODS

And we all know love is a glass which makes even a monster appear fascinating.

—Alberto Moravia, *The Woman of Rome*

. . . .

There are two ways to be fooled. One is to believe what isn't true; the other is to refuse to believe what is true.

—Søren Kierkegaard

Filipa had sought to reassure her charge, commiserating with Fisher over the shortcomings of the other guides. She wove a lyrical tapestry of their life together in eighteenth-century Theros. He visualized strolling down the cobblestone streets of the hamlet, past whitewashed houses and villagers leading laden donkeys to the market in the town square, bordered on one side by an imposing church named after the Emperor Constantine. The daily rhythm of provincial life was set against a backdrop of the heights of Thrace, the ancient land of Ovid's *Metamorphoses*, whose hearty sons filled the ranks of Alexander's army.

Fisher was unconcerned when he failed to locate Theros in the Greek gazetteers he consulted. The region had endured centuries of conflict, and many settlements in the region had either been destroyed or been given new names. Fisher fully expected that the evidence would be forthcoming when he had the opportunity to examine it firsthand in Greece: "The ultimate test was drawing closer. If Filipa could succeed . . . my love, my intuitive belief and my intellectual appreciation would be fused in delicious certainty."

After settling into his hotel after the flight to Thessaloniki, Fisher wasted no time making his way to the Institute for Balkan Studies, whose library was a veritable treasure trove of historical data about Greece. The solicitous librarian spent several hours poring through the Institute's collection of books, maps, directories and reports, searching for evidence of Theros's existence. Her efforts were in vain, yet Fisher persisted. Given the volatile history of the region, perhaps she had missed something?

He boarded a bus for the regional capital of Alexandroupolis, situated just forty kilometers from the Turkish border. Filipa had nostalgically recalled being there, trekking for days to reach the port city where the peasant villager was awed by "big, big, floating housings." His inquiries among the locals brought only blank stares, until a local priest recognized Filipa's family name of Gavrilos from his grandmother's village of Dadia, an hour's drive away up a nearby valley.

Fisher was electrified by what he learned next: The priest informed him that some of the residents of Dadia hailed from nearby Kotronia, "the village I had always suspected of being Theros under a new name." It was a long, sleepless night in his hotel as Fisher pondered the momentous revelation at hand. At long last, he dared hope, the long-sought proof of past lives was finally within reach. The convoluted rabbit trails of misinformation laid out by Russell and the other guides were now forgiven—indeed would be forgotten—now that Filipa was about to authenticate both her past life and the boundless love she shared with Fisher.

The next day Fisher boarded a bus for Soufli, a town on the Turkish border, where he rented a hotel room and caught a taxi for the last thirteen kilometers to Dadia. It was almost noon when he strolled into the sleepy town square. The locals seated in the shade ceased their idle conversation and stared at the newcomer. Fisher's clumsy pronunciation of Gavrilos brought no hint of recognition. Fisher was led to the town hall, where an English-speaking official confirmed that no one by that name lived in the town. Further, the official had never heard of a village by the name of Theros.

But there was one more glimmer of hope—always one more illusion to chase. The official recalled that his father had spoken of a place called "the holy ruins," which lay deep in the forest near Kotronia. The name of the site was Bukate. His interest piqued, Fisher pulled out his War Office map of the area and found Bukate marked in tiny letters. Fisher could scarcely believe his eyes: The site appeared to match Filipa's efforts back in Toronto to pinpoint Theros's location on a map of the area.

Fisher's renewed enthusiasm came up against a literal roadblock when he learned that the site of Bukate was located in a restricted border area. Once again the longed-for proof lay just out of reach as Fisher attempted to navigate the labyrinthine Greek bureaucracy. While awaiting the necessary authorization, Fisher toured the local sights, trying to quell the mounting waves of confusion and despair and dreading a looming epiphany.

Like the bursting of dawn upon those enveloped by darkness, the end came quickly. One evening, as Fisher sat with two venerable notables of the city over cups of Greek coffee, he suddenly felt constrained to share the great burden that belabored him, and opened up to them about his "metaphysical mission." He pulled out his tape recorder and played for them a section where he had asked Filipa to speak words of her native Greek. It was the moment of truth. Here were two Greek natives of the selfsame region where Filipa said she had lived.

One can only imagine Fisher's despairing countenance as the last vestiges of his great hope—and love—ebbed away. The men, having conferred with each other, slowly shook their heads. A word or two could be identified—yet again!—but in the main the recording was unintelligible. Upon hearing of his plans to visit the remote "holy ruins," one of the men smiled wisely, advising Fisher: "There is an ancient Greek proverb—only fools go to the forests."

Crestfallen, Fisher returned to his hotel. He was absent-mindedly glancing through some tourist brochures when the final straw hit him like a brick. One of the brochures stated that Alexandroupolis was founded in 1850. Suddenly Fisher realized the game was up: Filipa could not have walked for days to see the "big, big floating housings" in a city that did not come into existence until three-quarters of a century after she had allegedly died.

Fisher had caught Filipa in a "devastating anachronism," and "such outright dishonesty left me sick at heart and brimming with resentment." At that moment he realized that Bukate was just another fool's errand, and cancelled his plans to visit the restricted area. Fisher went for a long, heart-wrenching walk through the dark streets of Soufli, agonizing over the realization of his "irrevocable estrangement" from Filipa. His great, imagined love was lost, and forever gone.

Greece held nothing more for Fisher, and he began to retrace his steps back home. Late at night, as he awaited his return flight to Toronto, Fisher stared at the darkened ceiling of his hotel room. Two questions ran through his tortured mind: "First, after centuries of unsuccessful endeavor by minds far more enlightened than my own, how could I have been so arrogant to suppose that, with the guides' help, I was actually unravelling the mysteries of life and death? And secondly, if the guides were not guides after all, *who were they?*"

Masters of Deception

Fisher's plane glided into its final descent at Toronto Pearson Airport bearing a dispirited man, slumped in his seat. It was with considerable trepidation that he anticipated the confrontation with the guides that he knew must come. How could someone like himself, who took pride in his hard-won reputation as an investigative reporter, have allowed himself to be so deceived? His magnum opus, years in the planning, the work that would have established the reality of past lives, was now abandoned: "How could it be otherwise when the guides I had known and loved had metamorphosed from beings of light into masters of deception?"

The guides must be made to give an account of themselves. Russell had much to answer for. And Filipa—the very thought unleashed a veritable tumult of emotions. Complicating the anticipated meeting was the fact that Fisher would oppose the discarnates unaided. He had sent word on ahead to the group of his failure to confirm the earthly lives of the guides, yet none of the others was willing to accept the inevitable conclusion that he or she was being systematically lied to.

After a period of rest and reflection, Fisher found his fascination for the abode of spirits starting to ebb. He was gaining new appreciation for the real world. He tended his garden, reveling in the blooming flowers, the smell of freshly dug earth and the birdsong. Fisher felt that he was "coming back to earth," and for a long time it seemed that he had succeeded. But he would forever be a refugee from the world of spirits, which—he would learn to his great pain—did not take kindly to apostates.

The Fine Art of Obfuscation

Fisher's day of reckoning with the entities arrived. He made his way to Aviva's townhouse, steeling himself. Gone was the affable camaraderie: A gulf now separated Fisher from the True Believers, who encouraged him to continue looking for proof of the guides' past lives. As Michael Prescott notes, "The group members were so caught up in their shared fantasy that they could not tolerate the intrusion of facts and evidence."[1] Even Aviva had long overcome her earlier cynicism, and looked askance at the veteran reporter's findings. As she entered the trance state, Roger announced to Russell that Fisher had returned and wished to discuss his findings. "Yes, of course," replied Russell curtly. The battle was joined. Fisher laid out the evidence, or lack of it, explaining meticulously the absence of references in the historical records to Russell or Filipa, and a multitude of inaccuracies and discrepancies about names and places. Fisher, imagining that he had succeeded in making his case, was about to be schooled in the fine art of obfuscation.

Russell's first counterthrust was simply to dismiss Fisher's case, insisting that Fisher had failed to interpret the evidence properly, and thus had come up empty-handed. Fisher was so taken aback by Russell's arrogance that for a moment he began to doubt his own conclusions. Regaining his footing, he presented Russell with a specific example: the nonexistence of the St. Mary's Church where Russell claimed to have been buried. Fisher was attempting to do what is not humanly possible: pin down a vastly superior intelligence in a verbal contradiction.

Russell played him like a fiddle, describing a certain "traveling pastor" who had served the church, which, he claimed, was also a residence for a local family. At this point, the reader senses that the momentum had shifted subtly to Russell as Fisher attempted to process this new information. Once again frustrated, he changed the subject to other discrepancies.

And so it went, with Russell in every case dogmatically refusing to admit any error, instead offering alternative explanations for the historical evidence and introducing new details that Fisher was not in a position to confirm or deny.

Finally, an exasperated Fisher tried to cut through the dissembling, complaining that many of the basic facts were not confirmed even though he had double-checked the data given him by the guides. Russell retorted by turning the tables on Fisher, accusing him of allowing facts to get in the way of the truth: "When one closes one's mind, Filipa's charge, one must be very careful that one doesn't lock out all the good along with everything else."

Love Lost

Filipa! The hour was fast advancing and, caught up in the interminable discussion with Russell, Fisher had almost forgotten about the only one whose reaction to this enigma really mattered. He suggested that perhaps his beloved Filipa would like to contribute to the discussion.

Russell would have none of it. "No," he was adamant. "You've shut her out. You've quite completely shut her out. I don't think she'd have the energies."

Russell was now the cold arbitrator, the gatekeeper, between Fisher and Filipa. According to Russell, Filipa wanted to know what was more important to Fisher: to have all his facts in order, or to cherish and value the truth and love that the two of them shared? All the former bluster about rigorously "testing the spirits"—yes, even the guides' own words require scrutiny—was now forgotten. In the end it came down to the treacherous minefield of subjective feelings—the "truth in your heart."

And so it was that Russell played his strongest card in a shrewd ploy that appealed directly to Fisher's emotional attachment to Filipa, a bond cultivated through years of shared intimacies. He saw that Russell was expecting him to back down and plead to be reinstated with his beloved guide. But this final turn of the screw failed to have its expected effect, for Fisher had finally seen enough.

The confrontation between them raged. Fisher finally realized he was dealing with a surpassing intellect that was nevertheless incapable of admitting the slightest wrongdoing. The spell was broken. Fisher realized—though his understanding was far from clear—that the spirit entities in Aviva's living room came from a dark place rather than the realm of light. As Vincent McCann notes: "Although they often spoke of 'the good' for humanity, love, and 'forward development,' it became apparent that their true motives were to control and live vicariously through physical beings."[2]

Fisher was getting nowhere and decided to leave the field of battle. He walked out of Aviva's townhouse for the last time. He would never speak with Filipa again. But he would not—could not—forget. Years later he admitted that he still felt like the "disaffected lover" who pretends he never cared but still speaks of his beloved with terms of endearment.

Hungry Ghosts

Fisher determined that his research, originally intended to prove the existence of past lives, should see the light of day—albeit with a radically different thesis. *Hungry Ghosts* presents Fisher's hard-won realization that the guides were not higher-evolved entities dedicated to assisting humans on their spiritual path. He came to agree with Tibetan Buddhism on the topic, which teaches that the discarnates are mischievous "lost souls" trapped on a lower astral plane as a result of having lived base, selfish lives.

After the release of the book, Fisher received many letters from readers, some of whom disagreed with his views about the nature of the spirits. A former medium challenged his belief that the deceiving spirit guides were "lost souls"—spirits who might be unaware of their own deaths and are trapped between worlds because of ignorance:

> Compare this to the entities we have both experienced. They are masters of deception; they are articulate and eloquent with vast knowledge of philosophy at their disposal, whether fabricated or otherwise. . . . They have apparently limitless powers of precognition and access to any information they choose—past, present or future—enabling them, among other things, to impersonate whomsoever they wish with ease. This is not my idea of a poor lost soul stumbling in the darkness. The one thing I think we have both established beyond doubt is this: they are smart. They are very smart. Any lost soul this intelligent would surely have the ability and knowledge to progress to some higher state. If these souls are simply too evil to do so, and therefore have no knowledge of any supposedly higher realm, where do they obtain their vast understanding of philosophy? Not from living in a dark void trapped between worlds, that's for sure.[3]

Quoting the medium's letter in a revised and retitled work, *The Siren Call of Hungry Ghosts*, and calling her words "the most powerful, the most instructive, and the most damning of the practice of spiritualism," Fisher still could not bring himself to admit that the beings were an infinitely greater order of magnitude than mere wayward souls. This despite citing sources such as Johanna Michaelsen, who in *The Beautiful*

Side of Evil describes a sudden flash of intense hatred that emanated from a Spiritualist healer who claimed to channel an ancient Aztec writer.[4]

Fisher also admits that spirits and demons are presented in the Bible as cunning and deceitful beings, and quotes solemn scriptural warnings against them, beginning with the book of Deuteronomy: "Let no one be found among you who . . . practices divination or sorcery, interprets omens, engages in witchcraft, or casts spells, or who is a medium or spiritist or who consults the dead. Anyone who does these things is detestable to the LORD."[5] On many occasions Jesus Christ cast out "unclean spirits" and "demons." The apostle Paul warns that "Satan himself masquerades as an angel of light. It is not surprising, then, if his servants also masquerade as servants of righteousness."[6] The book of Revelation states that "those who practice magic arts . . . will be consigned to the fiery lake of burning sulfur. This is the second death."[7]

One suspects, in the face of such clear admonitions—which Fisher does not challenge—that some seductive compulsion was at work, enticing him into involvement with spirits. The letter of the former medium provides a clue, warning against "evil that hides beneath a façade of love and spirituality. . . . It is heady stuff that hooks you totally" but ends in "a Pandora's Box of horrors."[8] Her letter was one of many from individuals who had suffered terribly from mediumistic contact with spirits.

Elora Gorge

The demons would never release their grip on Fisher's tormented soul. He married and moved with his new bride into an ancient farmhouse in rural Ontario. But the years would not be good to Fisher. An accomplished journalist and author, with more than a million copies sold in 22 languages, he passed the next decade with no publication of note issuing from his pen. Fisher's life seemed to disintegrate slowly but surely. His health declined as a back injury curtailed his active lifestyle. Rumor had it that he was dogged by financial struggles. After years of escalating problems, his marriage ended in divorce. Fisher's use of antidepressants increased—medications that carried the increased risk of suicide.

Publication of *The Siren Call of Hungry Ghosts* and a new writing project were not enough to stay the overwhelming despair. Doug Williams deduces the root of Fisher's growing terror: "In his mind, vengeful demons had conspired to edge him prematurely towards failure, old age, poverty, and anonymity."[9]

And so it was that, at the age of 54, Joe Fisher drove to the Elora Gorge near his home in Fergus and followed the trail up to Lover's Leap. An aboriginal princess is said to have leapt from those limestone cliffs overlooking the Grand River after learning that her beloved had been killed in battle. There, on May 9, 2001, Fisher fell to his death.

Alexander Blair-Ewart, Fisher's publisher, spoke for many when he reflected: "Maybe at that point Joe decided that his life was so crappy—he was in pain, he was in debt, he realized that his relationships hadn't been good, and he just decided: OK, it ends here."[10]

But the speculation did not end there. On the Canadian television program "Supernatural Investigator: What Killed Joe Fisher?" Williams reported: "There are two mysterious details from the police accident report [referring to a photo of a skid mark]. This skid mark, perhaps made by Joe who fought being pushed over the edge, was noted by the police investigators. Its cause was listed as 'unexplained.'"[11] The police forensic report identified the mark as having been made by Joe's running shoe. There were no other identifiable footprints at the scene.

The second unexplained piece of evidence was a freshly broken tree branch at the site, possibly indicating that Fisher had grabbed it to prevent being pushed off the cliff by someone—or something. His friend Sheila O'Hearn observed: "It wasn't a clean jump. It seemed that there was some kind of a sliding motion, or there were prints that seem to have been left. And I think it was the broken branch that made people wonder."

In one of his last communications with Patrick Huyghe, his editor at Paraview Books, Fisher confided that the spirits were still harassing him for having written *Hungry Ghosts*. He had reason to be concerned. In an epilogue added to the revised version, Fisher wrote that shortly after completing *Hungry Ghosts* he was afflicted with an unexplained pain in his navel that stumped his doctors. The pain intensified for several weeks until, doubled over in pain, Fisher drove himself to the hospital, where emergency surgery was performed to remove a rare "malevolent growth, like an inverted pyramid, lying beneath my belly button."

In what Fisher took to be an ominous portend, within an hour of the surgery, he groggily picked up his ringing bedside phone. It was Claire, one of the members of Aviva's séance group, calling to inquire how he was. Fisher was taken aback—it had been years since they had been in contact. He asked her how she knew he was in the hospital, as he had not told anybody. She replied: "My guide told me." Fisher mused that "if [the guide] had told Claire where I was, perhaps he had put me there. Perhaps he was the source of this strange affliction which had baffled three physicians."

Shaken by his mysterious malady, which the doctors told him could well have been fatal, Fisher prayed for "deliverance so that the book could be completed." In an eerie premonition, he expressed his determination to finish the book "even if my onetime friends ultimately found a way to take my life." His friends would be left to wonder if his words were indeed prophetic.

There were other reasons for doubting that Fisher committed suicide. His friend, noted paranormal researcher and writer Colin Wilson, pointed out that Fisher had written a book warning against the taking of one's own life: "If the suicide could only realize the resulting intensification of difficulty which must enter the life to come, suicide would never be contemplated." Those close to Fisher could not comprehend how someone so committed to the doctrine of reincarnation would flagrantly disregard its prohibition on taking one's own life.

Other forces were at work. Fisher's mother may have been closer to the mark when she warned with trembling voice: "Demons. . . . You're talking to demons. And I don't like the sound of it one bit." Fisher clearly respected his mother's opinion about malevolent powers, which he mentions in a touching dedication to *Hungry Ghosts*: "This book is dedicated to my dear mother, Monica, who has always insisted that demons *do* exist."

Fisher was, however, forced to admit that his

metaphysical framework for living, lovingly and painstakingly constructed in recent years, was buckling under pressure. I no longer knew what to believe. Years of research had shown, finally, that mediumistic communication, for all its persuasiveness and plausibility, was fraught with duplicity.

Still, he could not bring himself to jettison his belief in the reality of past lives and reincarnation, choosing instead to dismiss his mother's naïve and outdated biblically informed viewpoint: "It was predictable enough, I suppose, leaping straight out of years of Christian conditioning."

Yet, as the former medium argued so emphatically, "misguided souls" was a wholly insufficient explanation for the nature of the guides. Could they be none other than the same irremediably evil beings, whose sole aim is the destruction of souls, that the Bible calls demons? Philosopher and paranormal investigator Jonathan Zap, quoting Shakespeare (Hamlet), suggests that the guides may actually have been one being, "a single shape-shifting entity who, like the devil, 'hath power to assume a pleasing shape' and was capable of performing a whole cast of characters of both genders."[12]

Whatever was responsible for Fisher leaping off the cliffs at Elora Gorge—whether his own inner demons or some external malevolent force—will never be known. His tragic story serves as a caution for those who, seeking the answers to life's deepest questions, are drawn to the "siren call" of entities from other dimensions.

THE MYSTERY OF CICADA 3301

Human beings are under the control of a strange force that bends them in absurd ways, forcing them to play a role in a bizarre game of deception.

—Dr. Jacques Vallée

L ate one evening in January 2012, a Swedish cryptosecurity researcher and developer named Joel Eriksson was trawling the web, looking for distraction. Little did he know that his life was about to intersect with what has been called "The Greatest Mystery on the Internet," which has confounded some of the world's best cyberhackers.

Browsing the bulletin board site 4Chan, against his better judgment Eriksson clicked on the notorious subforum *B*, a freewheeling site appealing to everyone from cutting-edge code breakers—the forum birthed the infamous "Anonymous" hacktivist network—to radicals thumbing their noses at conventional morality, to assorted sleazebags. The *Washington Post* notes:

> The board serves as a kind of catch-all/release valve for all the rape porn, self-harm pics, and creepy drawings of scantily clad children that aren't allowed in other forums. That is by design, too: 4chan technically bans trolling, racism and grotesque imagery elsewhere on the site, but permits it in /b/.[1]

There he spotted a cryptic message posted in stark white type against a black background:

> Hello. We are looking for highly intelligent individuals. To find them, we have devised a test.
> There is a message hidden in this image.
> Find it, and it will lead you on the road to finding us. We look forward to meeting the few that will make it all the way through.
> Good luck.
> 3301

Fair enough—Eriksson was game and had a spare hour or two. At first it was easy, at least for a skilled cryptographer like himself. The first clue was an example of digital steganography—concealing secret information within a digital file. Eriksson ran the image through a text-editing program, which yielded "Tiberius Claudius Caesar" and a line of meaningless letters.

He suspected this was a reference to an ancient encryption technique used by Julius Caesar. Since Tiberius was the fourth Roman emperor, Eriksson deduced that the number four was the key to solving the puzzle using the "Caesar Cipher," which indeed rendered a web address. He typed the link into his browser. A page came up with the image of a duck and these words:

Woops
   Just decoys this way.
   Looks like you can't guess how to get the message out.

The wording seemed odd. On a hunch, noting the juxtaposition of "guess" and "out," he decided to run the image through a decryption program called OutGuess. Up came a link to an obscure forum cryptically labeled "a2e7j6ic78h0j." Eriksson detected strange symbols that he identified as Mayan numbers, which led in turn to another cipher.

As Chris Bell, who investigated the story for the *Telegraph*, notes:

Suddenly, the encryption techniques jumped up a gear. And the puzzles themselves mutated in several different directions: hexadecimal characters, reverse-engineering, prime numbers. Pictures of the cicada insect—reminiscent of the moth imagery in Thomas Harris's *The Silence of the Lambs*—became a common motif.[2]

The mysterious series of seemingly never-ending ciphers, which came to be known as "Cicada 3301," challenged the abilities of even the most talented hackers and cryptoanalysts, many of whom banded together to pool their knowledge and expertise. The puzzles became increasingly complex and demanding, and required knowledge not only of cryptography, but also mathematics, data security, literature—from classical to cyberpunk—art, religion and philosophy.

The next level of the first Cicada 3301 riddle burst from the Internet into the real world when a hacker deciphered the code on the "a2e7j6ic78h0j" forum and discovered it was a United States telephone number. "Getting a phone number to call after solving one of the pieces of the puzzle was the first hint that this might not just be the work of a random Internet troll. This was definitely an unexpected turn,"[3] noted Eriksson.

Eriksson by then had taken time off from work to pursue the solution. The telephone number switched to a recorded message: The next clue, the robotic voice said, would be found in prime numbers associated with the original image.

Participants located the numbers and multiplied them together, yielding a website with a countdown clock and a picture of a cicada. Eriksson recalls: "This shared feeling of discovery was immense. But the plot was about to thicken even more."[4] When the countdown reached zero, the page showed fourteen GPS coordinates on four continents, including Warsaw, Paris, Seattle, Seoul, Arizona, California, New Orleans, Miami, Hawaii and Sydney.

What began as a network of online participants had now fanned out around the globe to the various coordinates. One by one, reports filtered back from individuals who had found posters pinned to lampposts bearing the cicada image and a QR code—a bar code designed to take shoppers to a website by using their smart phones.

Suddenly Cicada 3301 was bigger than anything a computer geek working from his mom's basement could possibly concoct. Whoever—or whatever—was behind the mysterious

Internet riddles had international reach. Scanning the images, hackers found that they were image URLs, which contained hidden codes leading to arcane literary references. One was a poem about King Arthur from a collection of pre-Christian Welsh manuscripts; another was cyberpunk writer William Gibson's 1992 poem "Agrippa (a book of the dead)"—a remarkable choice in that it was published on a 3.5in floppy disk that was programmed to erase itself after being read.

A Virtual Rabbit Hole

The search for Cicada 3301 was about to enter the darkest recesses of the Internet. An analysis of the QR codes on the posters revealed a TOR address. TOR—short for The Onion Router—is a gateway to the "darknet," the murky depths of the Internet that cannot be indexed by standard search engines. The vast darknet is believed to be up to five thousand times larger than the "surface" net, and harbors illegal activities, including human-trafficking rings, weapons dealings and terrorist networks, as well as government and military information. National Security Agency whistleblower Edward Snowden used it to leak files on government mass surveillance programs. The darknet's black marketplace, Silk Road, offers drugs and other contraband. Buying and selling are conducted using the digital currency *bitcoins*, which allows for anonymous financial transactions.

Only a select few would be permitted into the hallowed "inner sanctum" of Cicada. Then, unexpectedly, the TOR site closed down, shutting out Eriksson and many others without explanation save a final deciphered message: "We want the best, not the followers. Thus, the first few there will receive the prize."[5] Those fortunate enough to disappear down the cyber rabbit hole "went dark," leaving the world to wonder who or what was behind the increasingly complex riddles. One observer remarked:

It's a frustrating, enigmatic ending to a saga that, throughout, showed signs of careful craftsmanship and ingenious orchestration. It was a hunt that swept a room full of curious minds from an idle board on 4chan down the Internet's most anonymous corridors.[6]

But Cicada 3301 was just getting started. On January 4, 2013, a new message appeared—with a bizarre new twist. The riddle for the 2013 puzzle appeared on a Twitter feed: "Hello again. Our search for intelligent individuals now continues."

The complexity of the puzzle increased, requiring a stunning level of sophistication and breadth of knowledge across a broad swath of disciplines. One riddle included a photo from an old handwritten manuscript that could not be read by a computer, requiring specialized research skills to locate. Another riddle required participants to factor a 112-digit number, which took a high-speed computer seven hours to solve. A music puzzle required converting a song into a database of notes and then extracting a message, also in code. The decoded message turned out to include a peculiar religious reference: "Very good. You have proven to be the most dedicated to come this far to achieve enlightenment."

Questions were swirling: Why did Cicada 3301 choose to post the initial invitation on the notorious 4Chan/b/

subforum, which celebrates gore and shock porn? Also, what kind of group or organization would have the ability to place physical clues in countries around the world? Chris Bell expressed the view of many: "It is beyond the realms of my intelligence and beyond the realms of any individual's intelligence to do this."[7]

The Wickedest Man in the World

Another Cicada 3301 puzzle was posted in January 2014, which was found to contain further religious terminology indicating that the participants were being led on a quasi-spiritual quest: "Hello. Epiphany is upon you. Your pilgrimage has begun. Enlightenment awaits. Good luck. 3301."[8]

Participants discovered four pages from the "sacred" document *Liber Primus*, described as "an instruction book on how to transcend your own humanity, leaving your human-ness behind and evolving into a technomystical being."[9] The text mentions an iconic figure from the countercultural revolution whose name is already familiar to us: "Like Timothy Leary said: Learning how to operate your brain. Learning how to redesign chaos. Program your mind. Program reality."[10]

References to esoteric writers such as poet and Transcendentalist Ralph Waldo Emerson and English poet and painter William Blake appeared in the riddles. One puzzle presented a collage of Blake's paintings in an unusual arrangement that led some solvers to suspect that the collage was intended to represent a "Thelemic star"—a hexagram developed by none other than Aleister Crowley, the infamous twentieth-century occultist and self-proclaimed "Great Beast 666."

151

Crowley surfaced again when hackers discovered an enigmatic verse:

A book whose study is forbidden
Once dictated to a beast;
To be read once and then destroyed
Or you shall have no peace.[11]

The lines from *Liber AL vel Legis* (*The Book of the Law*) were penned by Crowley, who claimed the book was dictated to him over a three-day period in 1904 in Cairo, Egypt, by a "praeterhuman intelligence" calling itself "Aiwass." Crowley insisted that the message imparted by his spirit guide was beyond human capability and necessitated the supernatural intelligence of a higher order of being. *Liber AL vel Legis* announced the overthrowing of the Old World Order, which he considered to be dominated by a repressive Christendom. A New Age in the evolution of humanity had dawned, which Crowley called the "Aeon of Horus." The book is characterized by a decisive rejection of Judeo-Christian morality in favor of the charge: "Do what thou wilt."

Crowley's antipathy toward Christianity stood in stark contrast to his devout upbringing in Warwickshire, England. His parents were members of the Exclusive Brethren, an ultra-conservative faction of the Plymouth Brethren, which eschewed all "organized religion." Crowley respected his deeply religious yet moderate father, but his relationship with his more doctrinaire mother was strained, to say the least: She callously referred to her son as "the Beast" sent into the world to try her faith. Crowley resented the narrow and restrictive religious influence of the Brethren that he believed transformed his mother into a "brainless Bigot of the most narrow, logical, and inhuman type."[12]

At age ten Crowley was sent to board at Ebor School in Cambridge, a Plymouth Brethren prep school run by a strict disciplinarian, the Rev. Henry d'Arcy Champney. The students' days were filled with classes, followed by prayers, Bible readings and Christian service. Sunday was taken up with church services, with two hours alloted for other activities, such as the reading of books approved for Sunday. Despite the strict environment, the young Crowley wished desperately to emulate his father, and wrote enthusiastic letters home expressing his determination "to be the most devoted servant of Jesus in the whole school":

> I perceived a difficulty in the Scriptures. The beginning of my fall? I could not see how any one could be three days and three nights in the grave between Friday night and Sunday morning. I took my trouble to one of the masters, who admitted his own perplexity upon the point . . . he simply said that no one had been able to explain it. Then and there I resolved to astonish the world. Alas for boyish ambitions; the problem is still unsolved.[13]

Crowley's proclivity at Ebor earned him a prize for being at the top of his class in "religious knowledge, classics, and French." At age eleven, however, his world was upended when he was called home and informed that his father—the one island of sanity in his harsh, repressive world—had contracted tongue cancer.

Bowing to the leading of his Brethren community, Crowley's father declined the recommendation of surgery by one of England's leading specialists in favor of an "electrohomoeopathy" treatment by one Count Cesare Mattei. For a while things looked hopeful, but a year later Crowley, now back at school, had a disturbing dream about his father's death. The next day he was notified that his father had died the previous night.

A devastated Crowley was beset with questions, as noted by biographer Tobias Churton: "Burying the pain, he awoke into an anchor-less liberty. Something had conspired to kill his father; something was conspiring against *him*."[14] Complicating matters, his mother retreated further into dogmatism, joining a small sect of the Brethren that had separated from other Brethren over a doctrinal disagreement, which cut the family off from close relatives in the other faction. A bewildered Crowley was left to wonder how "people could number among God's chosen one day and collectively join the legions of the damned the next."[15] The bitterness ran deep, and would set the course of his life.

Crowley returned to school, but things had changed. Chafing under the harsh punishment brought on by his growing rebellion, he eventually left Ebor and spent the next several years being shuttled from school to school. Fortunately, he had inherited a large sum of money from his father, and when he came of age he abandoned the classroom for other pursuits, one of which was mountaineering. He scaled the famed peaks of Europe, then set his sights east to the Himalayas, where he participated in the first attempt to scale K2.

By this time Crowley had also plunged headlong into the black arts: Far from mere academic theorizing, his was a radical compact with evil, as evidenced by his declaration:

I bring you a positive and primaeval fact, magic by name; and with this I will build me a new Heaven and a new Earth.

I want none of your faint approval or faint dispraise; I want blasphemy, murder, rape, revolution, anything, bad or good, but strong.[16]

Crowley cast aside the Christian morality of his upbringing in favor of enticing words breathed in his ear by spirits in Cairo. The impious maxim "Do what thy wilt" became the herald call of the *Ordo Templi Orientis* (Order of Oriental Templars), Crowley's secretive occult organization that practiced "sex magick" rituals (*magick* being a means of effecting change through the occult). He boasted of being able to cast spells that would raise malevolent spirits, and championed the use of hard drugs, all of which earned him the well-deserved title "Wickedest Man in the World":

Crowley's lifestyle was absolutely shocking in the era in which he lived. Besides his interest in the occult, he was sexually promiscuous with both genders, . . . frequented prostitutes, was vocally defiant against Christianity and Victorian and post-Victorian prudishness toward sexual subjects, and was a drug addict. While Crowley detested Christianity, he considered himself an immensely religious and spiritual person.[17]

The bill for this Faustian bargain would come due, unavoidably. Already two of his wives had paid the price, having been driven by his moral anarchism to the insane asylum. Several of his multitudes of openly paraded mistresses committed suicide. Now at the end of his life, wasting away destitute in a boardinghouse in Hastings, South East England, abandoned by all but a few loyal followers, Crowley's sole remaining comfort was the astounding eleven grams of heroin he ingested per day, hundreds of times the dosage of hardened users.[18]

One wonders—let us ponder yet one more time!—what monstrous deception turned the young Aleister Crowley so violently from the Christian heritage of his forefathers, what another Englishman, John Bunyan, allegorized in *The Pilgrim's Progress* as the bright path leading to the Celestial City?

A Nefarious "Higher Wisdom"

The thread of occultism and the paranormal runs sinuously through Western society—at times nearly imperceptible when religious fervor and piety run strong. But "the god of this world," in the words of the apostle Paul, "has blinded the minds of the unbelieving."[19] The powers of darkness stand ready to emerge periodically from the shadows in the form of a willing minion such as Aleister Crowley.

Reviled by the puritanical Victorian society of his day, Crowley nontheless managed to achieve a renaissance decades after his death, as the societal transformation for which he longed has in many respects become a reality. Few could have imagined that the man who referred to himself as the "Great Beast 666" would one day be recognized by the BBC as the 73rd "greatest Briton of all time," or that his *Ordo Templi Orientis* would survive—even flourish. James Wasserman's *In the Center of the Fire: A Memoir of the Occult 1966–1989* documents the resurgence of the O.T.O. from fewer than a dozen members in 1976 to more than four thousand members in fifty countries.[20]

And here the circle begins to close, as the tentacles of Crowley's influence extend far beyond his lifetime to the icons of the countercultural revolution of the sixties and beyond. A picture of Crowley appears on the cover of the

Beatles' iconic *Sgt. Pepper's Lonely Hearts Club Band* album. John Lennon echoed Crowley's "Do what thou wilt" maxim when he summarized the philosophy behind the Fab Four's music: "The whole idea was to do what you want. Do what thou wilst, as long as it doesn't hurt somebody."[21]

We recognize another face on the *Sgt. Pepper* cover: Aldous Huxley, whose *Perennial Philosophy* sought to introduce the English-speaking world to the fundamental tenets of Eastern mysticism—ideas that had much in common with Crowley. Indeed, the two dined together in October 1930 in Berlin, and rumors persisted that Crowley took the opportunity to introduce Huxley to peyote.

What is clear is that Huxley shared Crowley's vision for societal revolution along the lines of The Beast's post-Christian Aeon of Horus: "Themes Huxley wrote about later in life, like drug glorification, parapsychology, and ancient mysticism rooted in the occult (practical magic and witchcraft), were introductory social-steps to lay the groundwork for the New World Order to emerge on a grand-unified scale."[22]

Timothy Leary did not make the cover of what *Rolling Stone* called "the most important rock & roll album of all time," but the omission failed to dampen his enthusiasm: "I declare that the Beatles are mutants, prototypes of evolutionary agents sent by God, endowed with a mysterious power to create a new human species."[23]

He might have been on to something: The Beatles themselves hinted at an inspiration behind their music that transcended mere mortals. Paul McCartney remarked that the group's music and lyrics would often come through in an hour or less. Yoko Ono stated: "Something did happen there. It was a kind of chemical. It was as if several people gathered around a table and a ghost appeared. It was that kind of communication. So they were like mediums, in a way."[24]

Leary sought "Higher Wisdom" in the Algerian desert under the ministrations of LSD, later discovering that he had "tripped on acid" at the same remote location where Aleister Crowley had ingested mescaline while performing occult rituals in an attempt to summon the "mighty demon Chroronzon." Leary would later state on national television: "I've been an admirer of Aleister Crowley. I think that I'm carrying on much of the work that he started over a hundred years ago. And the sixties themselves—you know, Crowley said, 'Do what thou wilt is the whole of the law.'"[25]

Crowley's influence was widespread: Led Zeppelin guitarist Jimmy Page, avid devotee of magick, purchased The Beast's former estate in Scotland along with artifacts from his life. More recently, rapper Jay-Z's clothing line, Rocawear, is replete with *Ordo Templi Orientis* imagery; he himself is pictured wearing a shirt emblazoned with "Do what thou wilt."

One of The Beast's celebrated modern-day admirers followed his drug habits to an early grave. Peaches Geldof, socialite daughter of Live Aid founder Bob Geldof, Tweeted about her new religion, *Ordo Templi Orientis*, urging her followers to read Crowley's books. She appeared in public proudly displaying her "OTO" tattoo shortly before tragically emulating the High Priest of Opiates by dying of a massive heroin overdose at age 25.

I Am Now Saved from Hell

In January 2013, a revealing message was posted on the code-sharing site and hacker hangout Pastebin. The anonymous writer, for whom English is not a native tongue, confessed to having been behind the scenes of Cicada 3301 for more than a decade. He began with a warning: "I'm here to warn you: stay away. This is a dangerous organization. While I agree with many of the goals, their ways are nefarious. In fact, I think it is like a left-hand path religion disguised as a progressive scientific organization."[26.] The term *left-hand path* was first used in Western occultism by Madame Helena Blavatsky to describe sex magick. Crowley also used the term, which is associated with the use of black magic, Satanism, Luciferianism and all things evil.

The former member goes on to describe how he was recruited, as a military officer, by a superior who gradually won his confidence over a period of more than a year: "Cicada gives knowledge to members slowly as they progress up the pyramid."[27] And what does this knowledge entail?

- They believe that there is no inherent meaning to anything. That all things are "empty and meaningless" and that "all things are always whole, perfect, and complete."
- They believe that within each person there is a "God." Not "God" in the sense of most religions, it is more like *Übermensch* in the writings of Nietzsche. They also see the Global Brain as another kind of "God."
- They teach that absolute morality does not exist.
- They teach there is no "real" reality. That all reality is dependent on the observer.
- They teach "There is no salvation in life; for there is nothing from which we must be saved."[28]

The former member conceded: "I believed this for a long time"—but then the real world intruded and swept away the false hope of "enlightenment." He found genuine love and meaning in the institution of the family:

> Now I am a father and husband. And I have come to search for the one true God and his son. This is why I have no choice but to leave this group who do not believe in Him. I encourage everyone to do the same. Worry not for your power here on earth, but only for your rewards in heaven. I am saved now from hell, and I ask you do same. Please read the Romans 10:13 and call on the name of the Lord.[29]

The enigmatic Cicada 3301 appears to be drawing participants inexorably into the dark web of the occult à la Blavatsky and Crowley. At the heart of the enchantment is the counterfeit promise of ultimate meaning through self-divinization, as expressed in the 2014 riddle:

> Welcome, pilgrim of the great journey toward the end of all things—it is not an easy trip, but for those who find their way here it is a necessary one—along the way you will find an end of all struggle and suffering, your innocence, your illusions, your certainty and your reality.
>
> Ultimately you will discover an end to self—it is through this pilgrimage that we shape ourselves and our realities—journey deep within and you will arrive outside—like the instar, it is only through going within that we may emerge:
>
> Wisdom: You are a being unto yourself—you are a law unto yourself—each intelligence is holy—for all that lives is holy.[30]

This message was echoed in another poem that was detected, entitled "The Instar Emergence":

Like the instar, tunneling to the surface
We must shed our own circumferences
Find the divinity within and emerge[31]

Here again we see the enticement of "You will be like God" first made in the Garden. The gauntlet has been cast; a clenched fist has been thrust heavenward in defiance of the Most High, at the sound of whose words all creation trembles: "See now that I myself am he! There is no god besides me. I put to death and I bring to life, I have wounded and I will heal, and no one can deliver out of my hand."[32]

Now let us see what can be said about this Paranormal Conspiracy that attempts to cast down God from His throne and install mortals in His place, with each man "a law unto himself."

THE ZOMBIE APOCALYPSE

What men do with real colors and substances the demons can easily do by showing unreal forms.

—Augustine

I t was a baffling discovery that perplexed archaeologists, leading to speculation that the walking dead are not just a plot device for horror films, and prompting the question, Were our Stone Age ancestors terrorized by the Undead?

The ancient settlement of Tel Qarassa lay undisturbed under the hardscrabble landscape of southern Syria for millennia until a Syrian-French archaeological team began to uncover its secrets in 2012. Excavating the graveyard at the site, the team discovered the skeletal remains of a group of thirty people—all buried without their heads.

That, in itself, is not unusual in the ancient Near East.[1] When the archaeologists later unearthed the crania in a nearby living space, however, they were taken aback to discover that the faces of each had been brutally smashed in. Even more enigmatic, it appeared that the skeletons had been exhumed years after their initial burial, and the skulls detached and mutilated at that later date. This led Juan José Ibañez of the Spanish National Research Council in Barcelona to suggest that

> these Stone Age "skull-smashers" believed the living were under some kind of threat from the dead. Perhaps they believed that the only way of protecting themselves was to smash in the corpses' faces, detach their heads and rebury them apart from their bodies.[2]

Could it be that, in the words of one headline, "Stone Age people may have battled against a zombie apocalypse"?[3] If so, this would explain the brutal smashing in of the skulls. Those familiar with the myriad of wildly popular zombie films and TV programs are likely to concur with *Zombiepedia*: "Nearly all zombie survivalists are in agreement that the destruction of the brain is the only surefire way to neutralize the zombie."[4]

We all know that zombies do not exist—at least not the wild-eyed, pasty-faced stiffs lurching toward you on the screen. But judging from the high-voltage popularity within our culture, might the zombie craze be tapping in to something very old within our brains—specifically, a primal fear of dark, primordial forces that stalk the modern world, just as they apparently terrified the ancient inhabitants of Tel Qarassa?

The Elusive Quarry

Powerful forces are making fleeting appearances at the edges of society in a cacophony of manifestations—shape-shifting wraiths appearing variously as humans, animals, large birds, sea monsters and any combination thereof. They lurk in forests and uninhabited places, linger in haunted houses and appear as the ghosts of the departed or as terrifying nighttime visages. Lately they have been appearing in the heavens in the various shapes of UFO crafts.

Ethnologists and anthropologists have given this multifarious phenomenon a name,[5] as George Hansen, author of *The Trickster and the Paranormal* explains:

> Briefly, the trickster is a character type found in mythology, folklore, and literature the world over; tricksters appear as animals, humans, and gods. They have a number of common characteristics, and some of their most salient qualities are disruption, unrestrained sexuality, disorder, and nonconformity to the establishment. . . . Like much of mythology, their stories appear irrational and are difficult to decipher into logical coherence. They have often puzzled scholars.[6]

Eminent cultural anthropologist Paul Radin describes the trickster as "an inchoate being of undetermined proportions."[7] From what we have already witnessed on these pages, it is clear that entities, adept at shape-shifting, are closely linked to the paranormal and the occult. They exhibit a level of intelligence and capability far surpassing that of mere humans, and, thus, it is no surprise that they can temporarily assume forms ranging from small animals to massive UFOs gliding through the night sky—and everything in between.

It is a grave error for mortals to assume that we can comprehend and thus control the trickster phenomenon. The sheer magnitude of the menace—what we have come to recognize as the Paranormal Conspiracy—defies human comprehension. In layman's terms, faced with the daunting capabilities of the trickster, on our own we do not stand a chance. Those who fail to recognize—or refuse to acknowledge—the unseen forces at work behind the scenes are often perplexed by the connections between the various paranormal phenomena:

> Ghostly phenomena have much in common with UFOs, encounters with demons, Bigfoot sightings, bedroom visitors, miracles associated with Elvis, and ET abductions. These experiences are sometimes accompanied by psi [shorthand for psychic phenomena] events, that is, ESP occurrences or macro-PK [observable phenomena such as the ability to move objects telepathically]. There is often overlap across these phenomena. Bigfoot sightings are sometimes reported in the same area as UFOs. Miraculous healings are reported as due to UFOs, saints, angels, and Elvis. Apparitions of the dead sometimes occur in UFO encounters. Poltergeist phenomena sometimes occur after ET abduction experiences. Deaths and disease are sometimes found with UFO contact as well as with demon infestations. Humanoids seem to display some of the characteristics of ghosts, Bigfoot, and séance materializations.[8]

Invariably tricksters remain shifty, indefinable, just out of reach. Whether they materialize as a UFO, Bigfoot or mediumistic communication with a departed loved one, proof of their existence remains sketchy and inconclusive. In *The Elusive Quarry: A Scientific Appraisal of Psychical*

Research,[9] Ray Hyman traces more than a century of investigation into the paranormal that began with the founding in 1882 of the Society of Psychical Research (SPR) in London. As the title indicates, Hyman documents the lack of repeatable experimental confirmation of the claims of parapsychology.

The SPR has had a long and colorful history studded with fraudsters employing parlor tricks, as well as the occasional case that defies rational explanation. While the argument rages among SPR members as to the authenticity of psychic phenomena, few if any could claim that the existence of the paranormal has been scientifically established.

The same dearth of indisputable evidence characterizes the work of J. B. Rhine, pioneer investigator of the paranormal and founder of the parapsychology lab at Duke University. Rhine conducted lab research and statistical analysis of psychic phenomena such as ESP and psychokinesis (remotely moving objects), and published impressive results that he claims to have achieved with his subjects. Once again, however—as it so often is with this baffling subject—the laboratory results that Rhine documents could not be repeated by other investigators.[10]

British paranormal investigator Tony Cornell, former president of the Cambridge University Society for Psychical Research and vice-president of the famed Society for Psychical Research, also found that paranormal episodes are rarely quantifiable. In his *Investigating the Paranormal*, the culmination of more than a half century of research, he found that "only twenty percent (of cases) are difficult to explain. And of those twenty percent, only a handful seem likely to be of the paranormal ilk."[11]

While the exceedingly low incidence of paranormal events that managed to pass muster was not sufficient to meet the threshold of proof, a geopolitical threat on the horizon forced a reexamination of psychic phenomena on a grand scale never before attempted.

The Star Gate Project

In the early 1970s at the height of the Cold War, United States intelligence sources reported that the then–Soviet Union was deeply involved in parapsychological research into clairvoyance (apprehending information through means other than the five known senses) and mental telepathy (transmitting information without sensory or physical interaction).

Alarmed by the obvious military advantages of gaining information about one's enemies from a distance and using psychic powers to communicate, a massive program to investigate "remote viewing" was quietly begun by the U.S. Defense Intelligence Agency and the Central Intelligence Agency.

Over the next two decades some twenty million dollars were spent on the clandestine project, which operated under the code name "Star Gate." The results of the research? As with the other cases we have examined of supposed knowledge gained through paranormal means, the Star Gate findings were oddly incongruent. On the one hand were the "eight martini" days, so-called because the remote viewing results were so spectacular that the team had to go out and imbibe with excess to calm down. But those days were too few and far between. In an independent evaluation of the program, the American Institutes for Research (AIR) concluded that the information gained through remote viewing was irrelevant, too vague to be useful—or clearly erroneous. The AIR report concluded that "continued use of remote viewing in intelligence gathering operations is not warranted," and in 1995 Star Gate was shut down.[12]

A Surfeit of Pseudo-Healers

The paranormal abilities that Star Gate investigated were put to the ultimate test when Russell Targ, co-founder of the project, faced a personal crisis. Dark currents ran in the Targ lineage: Russell's father owned an occult bookstore and published notable paranormal-themed volumes, including a biography of Helena Blavatsky and Erich von Däniken's *Chariots of the Gods*.

Targ's daughter, Elisabeth, had from her youth practiced extrasensory perception and "remote viewing." Trained as a psychiatrist, she continued the family tradition by investigating the possible benefits of applying psychic healing to AIDS patients and those afflicted with rare brain tumors.

In an extraordinary—and tragic—coincidence, at the age of forty Targ was diagnosed with the same deadly form of brain cancer that afflicted the patients in her studies. Once the shock wore off, she took it as the ultimate test of the efficacy of psychic healing. After the surgeon's knife failed to get all of the cancer, she announced stoically: "The next phase of the experiment begins," and began mobilizing her eclectic circle of paranormal contacts to direct their healing powers toward her.[13] From far and wide they came, determined to make Targ a definitive case study for New Age healing:

Her bedroom turned into a circus. Healers from everywhere showed up wanting to help. It was rarely peaceful and quiet. There was Phillip Scott, a Lakota sun dancer who burned sage; Nicolai Levashov, a Russian psychic who waved his hands; Harriet Bienfield, an acupuncturist with rare Chinese herbs; Desda Zuckerman, an energy worker who used techniques inspired by the ancient methods of the Miwok peoples. The reverend Rosalyn Bruyere phoned often, trying to get on Targ's schedule. And, of course, there was her father, Russell, urging her to meditate, calm her mind, go to that place.[14]

One man whom Targ felt "really had a gift" and could help her was a Druid who, unfortunately, had recently been deported to France. The soothsayer offered his services for a price, and proved to be a constantly shifting target. He agreed initially to help on condition that she assist with his immigration problems, then requested a job be arranged for him at the National Security Agency in counterterrorism, and, finally, demanded that Targ convince another family with a dying loved one to pay him $250,000 for his services.

More dangerous than annoying was the Russian psychic Nicolai Levashov, who urged Targ to cease radiation treatment, insisting he could stop the cancer telepathically. All that was needed, he claimed, was for the "necrotic cancer tissue" that was allegedly poisoning her to be excised by a special operation. Targ immediately ceased the radiation treatments that were ironically starting to take effect—after believing Levashov's claim that the positive effects were due to his spiritualistic ministrations.

The sad consequence of this hare-brained scheme was that Targ's new husband, Mark Comings, "wasted the last month of his wife's life on a wild goose chase, desperately calling every brain surgeon in the country, begging them to perform this surgery."[15] After one last desperate appeal to her alma mater, Stanford University, Comings received the reply:

> "We're sorry," he was told. "We've looked carefully at it. We disagree with what you've been told. The tumor growth is killing her. We can't do the surgery."
>
> "You're too late anyway," he returned. "She died last night."[16]

But all was not lost: Some of the selfsame mediums and spirit guides who were unable to draw from their infinite wisdom and paranormal abilities to heal Targ were quick to assure her loved ones with messages from the other side. One psychic healer wrote a letter to Comings about a vivid dream in which she observed Elisabeth appearing and saying something to him in an unrecognizable language. Comings took the letter to Russell and read it to him: "Targ instantly recognized the syllables as the Russian words for 'I love you.' Elisabeth was not only fluent in the language but had traveled there with her dad."[17]

And so the seductive allure of spirits from beyond the pale continues, boundlessly enchanting but never quite incontestable: a foundation built upon shifting sand. Does a phrase spoken in an unknown language—however impressive—compensate for the massive, collective failure of the psychic healers gathered around Elisabeth Targ?

The Binding of Satan

Why is it that, after more than a century of scientific investigation, the advocates of the paranormal have so little to show for their efforts? And why—as again in the case of Elisabeth Targ—do the discarnate entities continually fail to deliver on their grandiose promises?

The entities behind the phenomena are clearly in possession of capabilities far beyond human comprehension. Yet, as we have seen again and again, their power appears to be held in check. The entities are able to manifest themselves only partially and fleetingly, darting across the sky or stomping through the underbrush—yet never quite long enough for an unambiguous photo or video. Spirit guides speaking through mediums cannot seem to get their facts straight, even regarding rather straightforward matters of historical record. And they are unable to produce repeatable evidence of their existence in the laboratory.

The closer the entities' proximity to humans, the greater confusion and terror that they engender—as is the case with virtually all those who have experienced alien abduction. They do not, however, possess absolute control over their prey in that which matters above all else: the power of life or death. One would think it child's play for beings of such potency to rain down wholesale death and destruction upon the land; yet, despite the seething contempt for their quarry that the paranormal entities express, directly attributable fatalities are rare.[18]

The prologue to the book of Job sheds light on the limits placed upon the power of evil. In the passage, a conniving Satan presents himself to the throne of God, and hears Job described as someone who "is blameless and upright, a man who fears God and shuns evil."[19]

Satan demurs, claiming that the only reason Job fears God is because of the prosperity he enjoys: "But now stretch out your hand," he says to God, "and strike everything he has, and he will surely curse you to your face." To which the Lord accedes—with an important qualification: "Very well, then, everything he has is in your power, *but on the man himself do not lay a finger*."[20] After Job passes the test, Satan again accuses him before God, and the stakes are raised, but not before the Lord again admonishes Satan: "Very well, then, he is in your hands; *but you must spare his life*."[21]

Here we see two great truths. First, evil powers are not omnipotent. Second, God is.

Still, one wonders why beings of such magnitude are nevertheless incapable of uniformly applying their powers. Why could the competing psychics attending to Elisabeth Targ not "get their act together" and present a unified front that might have guided her to the right treatment? Similarly, we recall how the spirit guides in Joe Fisher's narrative got their stories wrong continually, and how the mediums guiding Percy Fawcett led him to oblivion in a dense jungle. Avoiding all of this should have been child's play for beings of such exalted intelligence and perception.

Here we must tread carefully, as such things are above human understanding, but a number of intriguing suggestions present themselves. The first is that the paranormal entities acquire their knowledge by assiduous observance of what humans say and do—but the knowledge so obtained is imperfect and can be erroneous. Theologians argue whether or not demons have the ability to read our minds. If that is indeed the case, then it would open a treasure-trove of information, which once again could be misguided or false.

Since the discarnates are not omniscient, they must rely on what they can gather by their powers of observation. Even though their capabilities far exceed that of humans, nevertheless, the ability to obtain information from a distance—such as facts about the former lives of Russell and Earnest in England or Filipa in Greece—would pose a challenge. If the competing—and contradictory—advice offered by Elisabeth Targ's psychic friends is any indication, one could imagine that the enmity of the demons toward one another is only surpassed by their hatred of those created in the image of God, thus hampering cooperation.

The inconsistent display of their powers may also be due to something very deep within the very nature of fallen angels and demons: overarching pride and arrogance combined with the determination to lead souls eternally astray. One can see easily how this would lead to indifference as to the consequences of the information provided, so long as the end result is achieved—and their human subjects remain subjugated to their will. This heartlessness was evident in Percy Fawcett's ultimate sacrifice in obedience to the discarnates.

The towering haughtiness and cruel nature of these beings might also drive them to push the limits of what the humans under their influence will endure while continuing to give obeisance to their spirit masters. The deeper their charges sink under waves of confusion and despair, the greater their perverse pleasure. The reader will recall how, in Joe Fisher's story, this effect was achieved with the others in Aviva's apartment, who continued to believe in Russell despite the compelling evidence to the contrary.

Finally, paranormal researcher and blogger Jonathan Zap offers a thought-provoking suggestion as to why these infernal spirits may be under constraint:

173

Perhaps the entities are compelled, by inner or outer causes, to include erroneous information so as not to overwhelm the free will of the human participants with revelations that are 100% verifiable. This could be explained as the mythic scenario of a demon under some sort of divine constraint to leave a calling card for the astute adept that shows that they are a diabolical agent.[22]

Miracles in the Storm

A revealing example of where discarnate spirits obtain their information is found in the experiences of a group of researchers, led by Mark Macy, who investigated Instrumental Transcommunication (ITC). In *Miracles in the Storm*, Macy relates his journey from agnostic to ardent believer in life after death after witnessing what he believed to be pictures and messages from the beyond transmitted through electronic equipment, including computers, video cameras, radios, telephones and television screens.[23]

Macy and the other researchers believed that electronically channeled entities were transmitting invaluable insight into the spirit world. The messages spoke of their (after)life on a planet called Marduk: a world of indescribable beauty where the departed led a peaceful and harmonious existence engaged in assisting less-evolved souls with their evolutionary progression.

Photographs of Marduk and its inhabitants appeared spontaneously on computers and video cameras—and here, as you might expect, is our very first clue. What are euphemistically described as "clear" photographs and depictions are anything but. One searches in vain—once again—for an example that does not resemble a camera hopelessly out of focus.

Even more telling is what happened to Macy's group. One would think that those honored with glimpses of a paradise where love has found its ultimate fulfillment would be inspired, even rapturous. Instead they were at each other's throats. Unable to work together any longer, the research group disbanded. Macy formed a new group that intensified the effort to maintain contact with their counterparts on Marduk.

New details would emerge concerning Marduk, which was described as a lush world watered by a single waterway, the River of Eternity. Among the transplanted earthlings on Marduk was nineteenth-century English explorer Sir Richard Francis Burton, who led an expedition up the river to regain control of the high-tech transmission center that communicated with ITC experimenters on earth. The center had been captured by a "negative spirit group" calling itself "Group 2105." Burton and his team counterattacked and succeeded in driving out the rebels.

If the exploits of a celebrated explorer on an exotic distant planet sound like science fiction, that is because it *is* science fiction. Macy's spirit communications bear an uncanny resemblance to Philip Jose Farmer's five-part Riverworld series, written between 1971 and 1983. Though the novels differ from the information provided about Marduk in many respects, they describe a futuristic world bisected by a single river valley that is inhabited by resurrected humans. A prominent character in Riverworld, as well as on Marduk, is Sir Richard Burton, who struggles against evil forces on each respective planet.

Did the spirits that described a futuristic utopia, complete with a hero with a famous name who saves the day, take their clue from a science fiction novel? Did they think no one would notice? Here we glimpse an unearthly hubris that knows no bounds, and actually thinks it can get away with such a flagrant counterfeit.

We will now examine the means employed by the sinister reptilian force behind the Paranormal Conspiracy to deceive and manipulate his prey—and how the diabolical attacks from another dimension may be utterly thwarted.

THE RESTLESS HEART

The hunger for love is much more difficult to remove than the hunger for bread.

—Mother Teresa

Theories abound as to the nature of and goals behind the Paranormal Conspiracy. William James, the great Harvard scholar and psychical researcher, remarked that God had made this phenomenon deliberately baffling.[1] He may have been referring to the fact that the forces behind psychic phenomena are in possession of powers that exceed human comprehension. James also recognized the valuable insights presented in Scripture, and suggested that the biblical understanding of the world of spirits deserved a more thorough hearing. In 1909, after publishing a study on mediumship, he made the following remarks, which are no less prophetic today than when penned a century ago:

> The refusal of modern "enlightenment" to treat "possession" as a hypothesis to be spoken of as even possible, in spite of the massive human tradition based on concrete human experience in its favor, has always seemed to me a curious example of the power of fashion in things "scientific." That the demon theory . . . will have its innings again is to my mind absolutely certain. One has to be "scientific" indeed to be blind and ignorant enough to suspect no such possibility.[2]

Hansen adds that, in addition to blindness and ignorance, one would also have to be foolhardy to ignore such a potent threat: "When the supernatural and irrational are banished from consciousness, they are not destroyed, rather, they become exceedingly dangerous."[3] The enemy is never so deadly as when he is invisible—when one has no idea of his whereabouts. The skeptic is like a willfully blindfolded man stumbling around a battlefield, insisting that the exploding rounds are flashes of lightning and claps of thunder.

The stories we have examined of those whose lives— willingly or unwillingly—intersected with the paranormal suggest a dual stratagem of the trickster phenomenon: fear and deception. Phenomena viewed from a distance, such as UFOs flashing across the sky or fleeting sightings of mysterious cryptids like Bigfoot, serve to disrupt the smug worldview of the witnesses. Even though it may have been a momentary episode, they are left with an unsettling sense of dread. It is as though they have experienced the living version of a cosmic billboard that announces: "You are not alone," and the flip side, "Deal with us."

The encroaching presence of the paranormal and occult in Western culture, if unchecked, will lead to a society in which the terror of dark forces is a way of life.

We have now entered the realm of the shaman, those "technicians of the sacred" found in cultures that are not grounded in the Judeo-Christian worldview. In practice, the inhabitants of such cultures live in fearful subjugation to the spirits; shamans assist with placating the spirits so that they do not cause harm. In *The Way of the Shaman*,[4] Michael Harner notes approvingly that the term avoids the "prejudicial overtones" of more traditional epithets such as *witch*, *witchdoctor*, *medicine man*, *sorcerer*, *wizard*, *magic man*, *magician* and *seer*.

And here the stark contrast with the Judeo-Christian worldview is clear, as several of these behaviors are condemned explicitly in Scripture because they constitute a fundamental disruption of the divine order, leading to chaos and decay. One need only look at societies in which witchdoctors, medicine men and wizards play prominent roles to see the point.[5] As noted philosopher of science Stanley Jaki pointed out, such cultures struggle to effect genuine human progress because their worldview does not support technological development. According to Jaki, belief in the Creator God of the Bible is the unique factor that has made modern science possible in the West.[6]

Contrivances of the Anti-Creator

The leader of the primordial rebellion against God—referred to as the devil or Satan in Scripture—burns with unquenchable hatred, knowing he does not, and can never, possess the divine power of creation. Thus, the one also called the Destroyer goes forth to do what is within his power: attack all that is good and entice souls to their damnation.

Theologians make a careful distinction between *supernatural*, which properly describes divine miracles, and *preternatural*, which refers to deceptive trickery and legerdemain. The devil and his vassals can do things that exceed what is possible for mortals in the material world, but they cannot exceed the limitations of their own created natures. In short, God can and does create *ex nihilo* (out of nothing); the devil cannot.

Two main *modi operandi* of this cunning artifice may be discerned. The first is a temporary and limited ability to manipulate or "bend" the laws of nature. Examples include levitating objects, unearthly sounds and apparitions. The manifestations may appear to be actual physical objects acting in time and space, such as cryptic footprints, UFO "landing pad" indentations in the soil or scratch marks left by an invisible attack—though the possibility of hoaxes must again be stressed.

The hallmark of this first operating method, as already noted, is that the ersatz materializations are fleeting and insufficient to provide inconclusive proof.

To answer the question "Are they real?" one can only suggest that these inexplicable phenomena are manifestations of *something*—psychic energy or whatever one wishes to call it—that does not have its origin in the three-dimensional universe but rather in an unimaginable mode of existence that Jesus referred to as "outer darkness."

The second *modus operandi* employed by the devil and his minions involves demonic virtual reality. By some unknown means a vivid scenario is imposed upon the mind, convincing the person that he or she has, for example, literally traveled to another location and experienced events that he or she believes to be real. Once again, one must keep in mind that we are dealing with beings in possession of knowledge about the working of the brain, knowledge that exceeds our ability even to grasp.

This demonic virtual reality has been observed in the laboratory. Dr. Rick Strassman, professor of psychiatry at the University of New Mexico, conducted experiments on the effects of DMT. The participants ingested the psychotropic drug under laboratory conditions while being monitored by psychologists. Once under the influence of DMT, the participants reported being transported to other locations and communicating with strange beings, etc. It is clear that their paranormal experiences occurred entirely in their minds. That is to say, the participants were not observed being physically transported to alien spacecraft or any other location; neither did any of the entities they described appear in the laboratory.

At the same time it was apparent that the experiences could not be dismissed as vivid imagination; participants from different backgrounds and cultures reported the same kinds of life-changing interactions with often identically described entities. This further indicates that the same spirit entities were manipulating various individuals, and were responsible for the similarities experienced by those individuals.

The Serpent Connection

The rebellion against the Creator that sought the downfall of humankind was instigated in the Garden by the one called the Serpent. There is a disturbing dark side to shamanism that pays homage to the reptilian enemy of God.

Harner lauds none other than Carlos Castaneda as having "performed the valuable service of introducing many Westerners" to the "sorcerer" type of shamanism.[7] Castaneda's books kindled a resurgence of interest in the age-old practice of trafficking with spirits, what the late Terence McKenna termed "the archaic revival."[8] McKenna was a leading proponent of using hallucinogenic substances to achieve altered states of consciousness. He had spent time in the Amazon participating in shamanistic ceremonies using ayahuasca, said to induce profound epiphanies regarding one's purpose in life.

After McKenna's untimely passing, Graham Hancock emerged as a prominent advocate of the use of DMT. Again, it is reportedly common for those under the influence of psychedelic drugs to encounter strange beings. One is struck by the creepy and disturbing visions of huge serpents, as described by Hancock:

> I journeyed deeper and then out of the patterns, and—formed out of them—appeared the beautiful, glittering, sinuous form of a serpent seeming to radiate compassion and concern for me and I sensed the presence of the great spirit, mother goddess of our planet, who I think of as Mother Ayahuasca, and I felt her healing energy.[9]

The oft-reported appearance of seemingly benevolent serpents to those under the influence of DMT brings to mind the ancient Hebraic equivalent of attaining "celestial consciousness": "You will be like God." And just as the true aim of Satan in reptilian form was the spiritual death of Adam and Eve, the serpents of modern-day shamanism are leading people away from the true God. It is the message of occultists like Crowley, who advocated the use of all manner of mind-altering substances for the purpose of worshiping and entering into communion with the "Snake that giveth knowledge and delight and bright glory."[10]

Just as Hancock was basking in the glow of the serpent's attention, a new wave of visions descended on him "like a storm," and he saw a figure to whom we have already been introduced:

> I was immediately in the presence of the entity . . . who I think of as "the Trickster" or "the Magician" or "the Sorcerer." . . . I do not know who this entity is or where he comes from. . . . My feelings of fear were very strong now, quite overwhelming and I wanted to flee, to run away from this scene, to open my eyes wide and stop the visions.[11]

Here again, we observe how even those who are advocates of shamanistic techniques cannot escape the instinctual fear of being in the presence of some great evil.

Shape-Shifting Entities

Paranormal researchers have remarked how the various phenomena "bleed over" into each other into what Hancock calls "multiple-interpenetrating dimensions":

> People in altered states of consciousness in the lab experiments in the University of New Mexico and deep in the Amazon jungle meet beings like this all the time. I've met them myself, again and again, repeatedly while drinking ayahuasca. And interesting enough, people who have the UFO

abduction experience very frequently meet hybrid beings of the same type who are part animal and part human. Often they appear first in that form before shape-shifting into the more familiar form of greys. . . . There is a universal human experience going on here, and our scientists are making a terrible mistake by just dismissing it all as delusions and hallucinations.[12]

What is troubling about this "universal human experience"— as has been amply documented—is that it commonly involves fear and deceit. While the entities are engendering terror in their victims, they are also practicing deception that has deleterious and sometimes tragic consequences. We recall the abject fear in Whitley Strieber during his abduction experiences: "Whatever was there seemed so monstrously ugly, so filthy and dark and sinister. Of course they were demons. They had to be."[13]

It is beyond understanding that those who insist that the entities—whether Strieber's alien abductors or Hancock's serpent—have noble goals behind their violent and obscene tactics, to which paranormal researcher Karla Turner replies:

Before we allow ourselves to believe in the benevolence of the alien interaction, we should ask, do enlightened beings need to use the cover of night to perform good deeds? Do they need to paralyze us and render us helpless to resist? Do angels need to steal our fetuses? Do they need to manipulate our children's genitals and probe our rectums? Are fear, pain and deception consistent with high spiritual motives?[14]

Of course they are not. In addition to the blatant physical violations of their victims, the entities also use a subtle weapon against the heart and mind: They exploit the innate human yearning for love and meaning for one's life. When the fanciful tapestry dissipates, the consequences can be devastating, as with Joe Fisher's lost spirit love. Faced with the pretenses of the spirit guides, he was forced to confront the utter collapse of his hopes and dreams: "How could it be otherwise," he asked, "when the guides I had known and loved had metamorphosed from beings of light into masters of deception?"

Fisher was the more easily misled because he would not face the possibility that objective evil exists in the form of demonic entities. He failed to look at the true nature of the trickster. As we noted, once he abandoned his biblical upbringing, he was left with a hodgepodge of Eastern mysticism and New Age beliefs, which consider such entities to be "troubled souls" or "mischievous spirits" that are trapped on a "lower astral plane."

Fisher's friend Ellison, a fellow member of the Toronto séance group, had his own chilling story of destructive manipulation by the guides, who attempted to destroy his marriage. Reflecting upon his own near-descent into madness, he remarked to Fisher that the entities

> often dazzled with their remarkable knowledge and acute perceptions but they had nothing but contempt for us. . . . Our communication allowed some light to shine into the darkness of where they are, and wherever that is must be God-awful in the extreme.[15]

Setting the Captives Free

Joe Jordan was about to stumble upon a powerful antidote to the machinations of the dark forces alluded to by Ellison and others. Jordan is a veteran UFO researcher who works with MUFON in Brevard County, Florida. After years of conducting field investigations, Jordan and his fellow researchers were frustrated by the lack of solid evidence. They began to have a nagging sense that there was something behind the phenomenon that was eluding them.

Jordan decided to get "closer to the source" and formed a research team to study cases of alien abductees. The first thing that struck them was the uniformity of negative fallout: "The one thing we saw was these people had symptoms of having a very traumatic experience in their life. The so called abduction experience was destroying lives and upsetting family relationships."[16] Moreover, many contactees seemed to have undergone a "conditioning process" involving transformation of their worldviews and involvement with metaphysical or New Age practices.

Jordan, however, would soon learn of those who underwent a spiritual transformation of a different kind—one that had a dramatic and powerful effect upon their abduction experiences. In 1996 he interviewed an abductee who described what had by now become the typical disturbing scenario of utter helplessness at the hands of malevolent beings. But then the man did something that Jordan had never heard before: "During his experience, which was terrifying, he was able to stop the experience abruptly. Being a Christian, he called out in the name and authority of Jesus Christ. He immediately woke up startled in his bed."[17]

Jordan was puzzled: This was the first time he had heard of someone actually stopping an abduction experience. He decided to contact a number of top abduction researchers across the country, and was surprised to hear that, without exception, each had come across similar cases. Also to a man (or woman), all of the researchers admitted that they did not report such cases because they feared it would affect their credibility.

Jordan was taken aback. As a veteran MUFON leader, he was well aware that the ufology community is rife with conspiracy theories and charges of government cover-ups. Yet here was a demonstrable suppression of evidence that could transform our understanding of the abduction phenomenon—by "the very researchers that we are relying on for the truth."[18] Jordan realized that there was a further reason the ufology community might keep the cases of spiritual deliverance quiet: These instances contradict the Extraterrestrial Hypothesis, which holds that UFOs are actual physical craft originating from distant galaxies.

After a newspaper article about his work was syndicated nationwide, Jordan was contacted by people around the country who reported similar deliverance experiences. He decided to dig further, and founded the CE4 Research Group to present stories of spiritual deliverance from dark entities, many of which have been posted on the organization's website.

The succinct but compelling case of Ginger typifies the dramatic release experienced by surprising numbers of abductees.

Ginger's brief but terrifying encounter began as she was taking a nap one Sunday afternoon in 1996. She was in the "lucid state" of not being fully awake when she suddenly felt tremendous pressure on her entire body. It was as if some creature was lying directly on top of her. She could not move and felt as though she was paralyzed: "I was on my back and feeling like I was being crushed."[19] Ginger felt "hot breath" and opened her eyes to the horrifying sight of a creature with reptilian skin and brown scales, with "green eyes looking into my soul":

> The monster pressed his face against mine, and out of his mouth came a hot red tongue. It snaked into my mouth and down my throat. My eyes locked on him and [I was] starting to choke. I couldn't believe what was happening.[20]

Ginger's account seems incredible but for the following: First, her experience is unfortunately all too common. Numerous cases that Jordan and his fellow researchers examined involved some form of bizarre sexual assault. Second, she recalls the event, which occurred seventeen years earlier, as though it happened yesterday. This in itself argues for an experience of much greater magnitude than a vivid dream or nightmare.

The spiritual attack ended as dramatically as it began. Ginger relates:

> I was like, "What is happening!" The first thought that came into my head was: "Oh Lord, Please help me. Jesus!"
> And then he was gone.

She concludes with the guileless affirmation: "This was real and it happened."[21]

Jordan reports more than four hundred—and growing—similar cases of those who were miraculously delivered from demonic assaults, demonstrating the truth of the biblical promise: "For there is no difference between Jew and Gentile—the same Lord is Lord of all and richly blesses all who call on him, for, 'Everyone who calls on the name of the Lord will be saved.'"[22]

The Enduring Quest

In the same Garden where the Serpent offered the enticement of divinity that resulted in spiritual and eventual physical death, we also find a great hope and promise for humankind. In chapter 2 of the book of Genesis we read: "The LORD God said, 'It is not good for the man to be alone. I will make a helper suitable for him.'"[23] As Adam receives his soulmate, the divine plan for marriage as the foundation of society is unveiled: "That is why a man leaves his father and mother and is united to his wife, and they become one flesh."[24]

This passage marks the inauguration of that wondrous adventure that we call love. The fruit of "they become one flesh" reverberates through the ages—and beyond, yea into eternity. It is rooted in the family, that warm hearth where love is nourished and learned by children who emulate the affection between their father and mother in their own lives, and share it beyond to the community and the world. For love, like its divine Author, cannot be confined, and provides the impetus for philanthropy and charitable work everywhere. In the words of Jesus, "No one lights a lamp and puts it in a place where it will be hidden."[25]

It is a grand plan too marvelous for mortals to comprehend. The evil one has seen more, having been cast from heaven for attempting to seize the very throne of God: "Woe to the earth and the sea, because the devil has come down to you, having great wrath, knowing that he has only a short time."[26] The Destroyer wars with undying hatred against all that is good—beginning with the divinely ordained family.

We have seen much on these pages about the universal longing for love and ultimate meaning—a quest that Satan seeks to divert from Bunyan's bright path to the Celestial City to dark byways and shadowy realms. For some, a familial wounding sets the tragic course of their lives. The young Percy Fawcett was driven to achieve—playing through despite having his front teeth knocked out—determined to be the man his dissolute father never was, and to earn the approval of his distant mother.

Helena Blavatsky's dysfunctional upbringing doubtlessly played a part in her early fascination with occultism. Similarly, a youthful Aleister Crowley, set adrift by the death of his kindly father and left to the vicissitudes of his mother's harsh, unbalanced faith, embraced a draconian rejection of Christianity.

The young Carlos Castaneda's loss of his beloved mother profoundly affected him. His wife, Margaret, wrote that when his mother died "Carlos was grief stricken. He refused to attend the funeral and locked himself in his room for three days without eating."[27] He became obsessed with moving to the United States, where a new life—and don Juan—awaited.

Joe Fisher succumbed to that ever-elusive pursuit of romance that so often mimics and poses as genuine love, like a beautifully wrapped gift that inside is empty. Having jettisoned the bulwark of his Christian upbringing, he had no defense against the intricate tapestry woven by lying spirits.

Weary of the tiresome mendacity, we turn for refuge once again to the inspiring story of John and Hilda Silva. Theirs was a union rooted in mutual faith, and exemplified the self-giving love whose source is God. We are reminded of the words of the Church Father Augustine of Hippo, "You have made us for yourself, O Lord, and our heart is restless until it rests in you."[28]

Augustine spent many years searching for love and meaning, including engaging in hedonism as a youth. He was also a follower of the Manichaean religion, which taught reincarnation. Through the intercessions of his devout mother, Monica, Augustine came to faith in Christ. Instead of endless cycles of birth and rebirth, interspaced with sojourning on astral planes, like John and Hilda long after him Augustine came joyfully to anticipate life ever after in the heavenly City of God.

Though the evil one may appear to succeed for a season, his end is certain: "And the devil, who deceived them, was thrown into the lake of burning sulfur, where the beast and the false prophet had been thrown. They will be tormented day and night for ever and ever."[29]

What will remain is love, resplendent and boundless in the glorious world to come, where those who love Him will reign forever. Thus will human history end—and eternity begin.

And so also concludes our inquiry into the Paranormal Conspiracy against the souls of men and women with the confidence that there is One who is greater than the dark, malevolent forces that have only fear, chaos and hopelessness to offer. Let us take great comfort in the admonition of the apostle Paul:

See to it that no one takes you captive through hollow and deceptive philosophy, which depends on human tradition and the elemental spiritual forces of this world rather than on Christ. For in Christ all the fullness of the Deity lives in bodily form, and in Christ you have been brought to fullness. He is the head over every power and authority.[30]

Amen!

NOTES

Chapter 1: Doctrines of Demons

1. James Robertson, "EXCLUSIVE—The true love story of the widower who dined at a burger bar with his wife's picture: 'I carry her photo everywhere and tell her how much I love her. I'm waiting for the day we can be together forever,'" *Mail Online*, October 31, 2014, http://www.dailymail.co.uk/news/article-2815098/I-m-just-waiting-day -comes-forever-Widower-broke-hearts-pictured-dining-picture-woman-loved-55-years -tells-MailOnline-extraordinary-love-story.html#ixzz3NugVPbDq.

2. Ibid.

3. Kelli Bender, "Widower Keeps Late Wife's Memory Alive by Dining with Her Photo," *Huffington Post*, October 30, 2014, http://www.people.com/article/man-dines -with-photo-of-late-wife.

4. Viktor Frankl, *Man's Search for Meaning* (New York: Washington Square Press, 1963), 58.

5. Ibid., 58–59.

6. 1 John 4:8.

7. 1 Peter 5:8.

8. Revelation 2:27 NASB.

9. Matthew 4:10.

10. Matthew 4:11.

11. Revelation 12:12.

12. John 8:44.

13. 1 Timothy 4:1.

14. Genesis 3:5.

15. Ephesians 2:2.

16. Kurt Vonnegut, "The Mysterious Madam Blavatsky," *McCall's*, March 1970, quoted in Gary Lachman, *Madam Blavatsky: The Mother of Modern Spirituality* (New York: Penguin, 2012), 10.

17. Philippians 2:9.

Chapter 2: The Doors of Perception

1. Aldous Huxley, *The Doors of Perception* (New York: Harper, 1954).
2. Dana Sawyer, *Aldous Huxley, a Biography* (New York: Crossroad, 2002), 147.
3. Gary Lachman, *Turn Off Your Mind: The Mystic Sixties and the Dark Side of the Age of Aquarius* (New York: Disinformation, 2001), 8–9.
4. Carlos Castaneda, *The Teachings of Don Juan: A Yaqui Way of Knowledge* (Oakland: University of California Press, 1968).
5. Unless otherwise indicated, subsequent quotations referencing Carlos Castaneda included in this chapter are taken from: Carlos Castaneda, *Journey to Ixtlan: The Lessons of Don Juan* (New York: Simon & Schuster, 1972).
6. Margaret Runyan Castaneda, *My Magical Journey with Carlos Castaneda* (Lincoln, Neb.: iUniverse, 2001), vii.
7. Ibid., 15.
8. Richard de Mille prepared timelines of Castaneda's first three books showing that the events described could not have plausibly occurred in the order stated. See Richard de Mille, *Castaneda's Journey: The Power and the Allegory* (Santa Barbara, Calif.: Capra Press, 1976).
9. Runyan Castaneda, *Magical Journey*, 31.
10. Sandy McIntosh, "Book Review," Sustained Action, 1999, http://www.sustained action.org/Explorations/margaret_runyan_bookreview.htm.
11. Peter Applebome, "Carlos Castaneda, Mystical and Mysterious Writer, Dies," *New York Times*, June 20, 1998, http://www.nytimes.com/1998/06/20/arts/carlos -castaneda-mystical-and-mysterious-writer-dies.html.

Chapter 3: Beings of High Strangeness

1. Christopher Munch, "Sasquatch and Us," *YouTube*, October 28, 2012, http:// www.youtube.com/watch?v=Bjj—hAufig.
2. A doctoral candidate at Pennsylvania State University mapped every sighting compiled by BFRO. See: Joshua Stevens, "'Squatch Watch: 92 Years of Bigfoot Sightings in the US and Canada," *Joshua Stevens*, September 17, 2013, http://www .joshuastevens.net/visualization/squatch-watch-92-years-of-bigfoot-sightings-in -us-and-canada/.
3. "Large Animals Recently Discovered: Bili Apes and Giant Fresh Water Stingray," *Bigfoot Evidence*, January 4, 2013, http://bigfootevidence.blogspot.com/2013/01/large -animals-recently-discovered-bili.html.
4. "Large Mystery Primate Discovery Should Silence Skeptics," *Team Tracker Bigfoot News,* June 18, 2013, http://bigfootevidence101.blogspot.com/2013/06/large -mystery-primate-discovery-should_18.html.
5. "Mystery Apes Are Chubby Chimps, Zoologists Find," ABC News Online—Sci Tech, June 29, 2006, http://www.abc.net.au/science/news/scitech/SciTechRepublish _1674285.htm.
6. "The Bondo Mystery Apes: What exactly has Karl found in the DRC?" Karl Ammann.com, 2014, http://www.karlammann.com/bili.php#.U83ILDRdU-X.
7. "World Wildlife Fund: Species: Gorilla," http://www.worldwildlife.org/species/ gorilla.
8. "10 Reasons Why Bigfoot's a Bust," *Discovery News Magazine*, May 26, 2014, http://news.discovery.com/animals/endangered-species/10-reasons-why-bigfoots-a -bust-140526.htm.

9. Ibid.

10. H. Kühl, F. Maisels, M. Ancrenaz, and E.A. Williamson, "Best Practice Guidelines for Surveys and Monitoring of Great Ape Populations," *International Union for Conservation of Nature: Occasional Paper of the IUCN Species Survival Commission*, no. 36 (2007), http://www.primate-sg.org/storage/pdf/BP.surveys.pdf.

11. Ibid., 13.

12. Kathy Moskowitz, U.S.D.A. Forest Service, "An Analysis of an Alleged Sasquatch Nest," Bigfoot Field Research Organization, 2014, http://www.bfro.net/ref/fieldres/sasquatchnest.asp.

13. Ibid.

14. Ibid. A Google search brings up a number of other suggested Bigfoot nests, neither of which offers indisputable evidence like that found, for example, at great ape nesting sites. "Open-minded but skeptical" commentator Micah Hanks offers a simpler explanation: "While proponents of Bigfoot's existence would argue they are similar to nesting areas constructed by primates, in most cases they just as easily could have been prepared by bears." Micah Hanks, "Mysterious Bigfoot 'Nests': Another Explanation?" *Gralien Report*, December 17, 2010, http://gralienreport.com/about/.

15. Stevens, "'Squatch Watch."

16. Ibid.

17. Greg Long, *The Making of Bigfoot: The Inside Story* (Amherst, N.Y.: Prometheus, 2004).

18. Joe Nickell, "Bigfoot Legend, Bob Gimlin," *Center for Inquiry: Investigative Briefs with Joe Nickell*, http://www.centerforinquiry.net/blogs/entry/bigfoot_legend_bob_gimlin/.

19. "Monsters and Mysteries in America: Alien Bigfoot, Cajun Werewolf, Lake Pepin Monster," *Destination America*, aired March 14, 2014.

20. Jeffery Pritchett, "Sasquatch and UFOs and the high strange connection: 'Interview with Stan Gordon,'" *Examiner*, May 2, 2012, http://www.examiner.com/article/sasquatch-and-ufos-and-the-high-strange-connection-interview-with-stan-gordon. See also, Stan Gordon, *Silent Invasion: The Pennsylvania UFO-Bigfoot Casebook*, Stan Gordon Productions, October 30, 2010.

21. Jeffery Pritchett, "Interview with Barton Nunnelly on the Inhumanoids and Bigfoot in Kentucky," *Examiner*, June 1, 2012, http://www.examiner.com/article/interview-with-barton-nunnelly-on-the-inhumanoids-and-bigfoot-kentucky.

22. Pritchett, "Sasquatch and UFOs."

Chapter 4: Messengers of Deception

1. John Kelly, "The month that E.T. came to D.C.," *Washington Post*, July 20, 2012, http://www.washingtonpost.com/local/the-month-that-et-came-to-dc/2012/07/20/gJQAZp2ayW_story.html.

2. Jerome Clark, *The UFO Book: Encyclopedia of the Extraterrestrial* (Canton, Mich.: Visible Ink, 1998), 656.

3. B. J. Booth, "1952 Washington D.C. Sightings," *UFO Casebook*, http://www.ufocasebook.com/washingtondc1952.html.

4. George Adamski, *Flying Saucers Have Landed* (London: Thomas Werner Laurie, 1953), 134–135.

5. Robert Hastings, *UFOs and Nukes: Extraordinary Encounters at Nuclear Weapons Sites* (Bloomington, Ind.: Author House, 2008), Kindle edition.

6. Robert Hastings, "Front Page News in the *Washington Post*: UFOs Hovered Over Nuclear Missile Sites," *UFOs and Nukes*, March 12, 2013, http://www.ufohastings.com/articles/front-page-news-in-the-washington-post.

7. Hastings, *UFOs and Nukes: Extraordinary Encounters*.

8. Brian Koberlein, "How Big Is the Universe?" *Universe Today*, August 11, 2014, http://www.universetoday.com/113786/how-big-is-the-universe-2/.

9. Jerome Clark, *The UFO Encyclopedia: The Phenomenon from the Beginning* (Detroit: Omingraphics, 1998), 28.

10. "Fermi Paradox," SETI Institute, 2015, http://www.seti.org/seti-institute/project/details/fermi-paradox.

11. Erik A. Petigura, Andrew W. Howard, and Geoffrey W. Marcy, "Prevalence of Earth-size planets orbiting Sun-like stars," *Proceedings of the National Academy of Science*, no. 48 (November 4, 2013). Note: The Kepler Space Observatory is now disabled.

12. "What are the chances of life existing outside our solar system?" NASA Goddard Space Flight Center—Ask an Astrophysicist, December 5, 2014, http://imagine.gsfc.nasa.gov/docs/ask_astro/answers/970924.html.

13. "Fermi Paradox."

14. "The Largest Star Currently Known," *Sidewalk Astronomy*, April 8, 2013, http://sidewalkastronomy.ca/the-largest-star-currently-known/.

15. "How Big Is Our Universe," NASA Office of Space Science, July 15, 2014, http://www.nasa.gov/audience/foreducators/5–8/features/F_How_Big_is_Our_Universe.html.

16. Erik Van Datiken, "8 Most Common UFO Shapes," *Weekly World News*, April 13, 2009, http://weeklyworldnews.com/aliens/7556/8-most-common-ufo-shapes/3/.

17. John Rimmer, "Evaluating the Abductee Experience," in *Phenomenon: Forty Years of Flying Saucers*, ed. John Spencer and Hilary Evans (New York: Avon, 1988), 167.

18. Peter Hough, "The Development of UFO Occupants," in *Phenomenon*, ed. Spencer and Evans, 27.

19. Carl Sagan, *The Demon-Haunted World: Science as a Candle in the Dark* (London: Headline, 1997), 95.

20. John Mack, *Abduction: Human Encounters with Aliens* (New York: Scribner, 2007), 48.

21. John Keel, *The Mothman Prophecies* (New York: Saturday Review Press, 1975).

22. John Keel, *Operation Trojan Horse* (New York: Putnam, 1970), 183.

23. Jacques Vallée, *Revelations: Alien Contact and Human Deception* (New York: Ballantine, 1991), 266.

24. John 3:19–20 NASB.

25. Ephesians 6:12.

26. Keel, *Operation Trojan Horse*, 247.

27. Keel, *Operation Trojan Horse*, 299.

28. Karla Turner, *Taken: Inside the Alien-Human Abduction Agenda* (Roland, Ark.: Kelt Works, 1994), 4. Hastings (*UFOs and Nukes: Extraordinary Encounters*) concurs: "It must be acknowledged that, at the moment, irrefutable scientific evidence relating to the nature of the phenomenon—which would settle the issue once and for all—remains elusive."

29. Hastings, *UFOs and Nukes: Extraordinary Encounters*.

30. Turner, *Taken*, 9.

Chapter 5: Unearthly Encounters

1. Whitley Strieber, *Communion* (New York: Avon, 1987).

2. Budd Hopkins, *Intruders: The Incredible Visitations at Copley Woods* (New York: Ballantine, 1987); Budd Hopkins, *Missing Time* (New York: Ballantine, 1987).

3. Strieber, *Communion*, 11.

4. Ibid.

5. Ibid.

6. Ibid., 16.

7. Ibid., 20.

8. Ibid., 21.

9. Ibid.

10. Walt Andrus, in discussion with the author, September 9, 1994.

11. Whitley Strieber, *Transformation: The Breakthrough* (New York: Avon, 1988), 44–45.

12. Ibid., 140.

13. Whitley Strieber, "Shedding Light on the Dark Side, Part Two" *Unknown Country—Whitley's Journal*, December 7, 2003, http://www.unknowncountry.com /journal/shedding-light-dark-side-part-two.

14. Aeolus Kephas [Jason Horsley], "Through a Fractured Glass, Darkly, Part One: The Facts in the Strange Case of Whitley Strieber," *Reality Sandwich*, March 30, 2012, http://realitysandwich.com/142495/strange_case_whitley_strieber_1/.

15. Anne Strieber and Whitley Strieber, *Miraculous Journey* (Hertford, N.C.: Crossroad Press, 2014), Kindle edition.

16. Ibid.

17. Ibid.

18. Ibid. Note: Anne Strieber made what Whitley called a "miraculous recovery" and resumed writing on their website unknowncountry.com. A decade later, however, she suffered another stroke, which left her partially incapacitated.

19. Ibid.

20. C. D. B. Bryan, *Close Encounters of the Fourth Kind* (New York: Penguin, 1996).

21. Ibid., 301.

22. Ibid., 362.

23. Ibid., 400.

24. Ralph Blumenthal, "Alien Nation: Have Humans Been Abducted by Extraterrestrials?" *Vanity Fair*, May 10, 2013, http://www.vanityfair.com/culture/2013/05/ americans-alien-abduction-science.

Chapter 6: The Lost City of Z

1. Misha Williams, *AmaZonia*, April 15, 2004, http://www.fawcettsamazonia .co.uk/pdf/AmaZonia%20by%20Misha%20Williams.pdf.

2. Ibid.

3. David Grann, *The Lost City of Z: A Tale of Deadly Obsession in the Amazon* (New York: Doubleday, 2009).

4. Simon Bendle, "Percy Fawcett: Zed or Dead," in *Great British Nutters*, February 13, 2013, http://greatbritishnutters.blogspot.com/2013/02/percy-fawcett-zed-or-dead .html.

5. Grann, *The Lost City of Z*.

6. Ibid. It was not uncommon in séances for the "departed" to conveniently express his or her regrets from beyond the grave for doubting the new Spiritualist faith. In Kingsley's case, he had been a devout Christian and was presumably taking the opportunity to ask his father's forgiveness for having opposed his involvement in Spiritualism.

7. Duncan J. D. Smith, "The Hunt for Colonel Fawcett," 2010, http://www.penguin cerisetravel.com/travellers/PERCY%20FAWCETT%20BIO.pdf?phpMyAdmin =46fbfa79d18d8a22f175f98980539360.

8. Williams reports: "Currently, one young member of the Kalapalos tribe openly admits that the Vilas Boas brothers wrote the whole script for this hoax and had tried to pass off the skeleton of their elder as Fawcett's remains and claims his people now want the skeleton back from where it is stored today, in a medical school in Sao Paulo." See: Williams, *AmaZonia*.

Chapter 7: The Great Scheme

1. David Grann relates his similar experience of being shown the Secret Papers in the home of Fawcett's granddaughter: "She led me into a back room and opened a large wooden trunk. Inside were several leather-bound books. Their covers were worn and tattered, their bindings breaking apart. Some were held together only by strings, tied in bows. 'What are they?' I asked. 'PHF's diaries and logbooks.' She handed them to me. 'You can look through them, but you must guard them carefully.'" See: Grann, *The Lost City of Z*.

2. Williams, *AmaZonia*.

3. John Michael Greer, *Atlantis: Ancient Legacy, Hidden Prophecy* (Woodbury, Minn.: Llewellyn Worldwide, 2007), 49.

4. Marion Meade, *Madame Blavatsky: The Woman behind the Myth* (Open Road Media, April 1, 2014), Google eBook.

5. Quoted by Grann, *The Lost City of Z*.

6. Grann, *The Lost City of Z*.

7. "Blavatsky, Helena Petrovna (1831–1891)," *The Mystica—an on-line encyclopedia of the occult, mysticism, magic, paranormal and more*, http://www.themystica.com /mystica/articles/b/blavatsky_helena_petrovna.html.

8. Ibid.

9. Questions have been raised as to whether or not Blavatsky's illustrious escapades in the East ever took place. See: Martin Brauen, *Dreamworld Tibet: Western Illusions* (Trumbull, Conn.: Weatherhill, 2004), 26, http://www.scribd.com/doc /217806829/202282660-Dreamworld-Tibet-Western-Illusions-pdf: "Although the Theosophists have tried time and again to provide evidence for a long stay by HPB in Tibet—altogether she is supposed to have spent seven years there—it remains beyond doubt, not only that she never lived in the neighborhood of Tashi Lhünpo, but even that she probably never trod on actual Tibetan soil." Brauen allows that "there are certain indications that HPB stayed in the region of Darjeeling and reached as far as Sikkim, where she met Tibetans and Bhutanese."

10. Brauen, *Dreamworld Tibet*.

11. Ibid.

12. William Emmette Coleman, "The Sources of Madame Blavatsky's Writings," first published in Vsevolod Sergyeevich Solovyoff, *A Modern Priestess of Isis* (London: Longmans, Green, and Co., 1895), Appendix C, 353–366, http://www.blavatskyarchives .com/colemansources1895.htm.

13. Donald S. Lopez, *Prisoners of Shangri-La: Tibetan Buddhism and the West* (Chicago: University of Chicago Press, 1998), 86.

14. Ibid.

15. Ibid.

16. Ibid.

17. Ibid.

18. Grann, *The Lost City of Z*.

19. Williams, *AmaZonia*.

20. Brian Fawcett, *Exploration Fawcett: Lt. Colonel P H arranged from his manuscripts, letters, log-books, and records* (London: Hutchinson, 1953). The book became a bestseller and has been reprinted as recently as 2010. Subsequent reprints assume the book was ghost written by Brian and credit him as author.

21. Williams, *AmaZonia*. In another example, Brian relates how M assisted him in perpetrating the false Fawcett story when he was interviewed by BBC Television.

22. Ibid.

23. Brian Fawcett, *Ruins in the Sky* (London: Hutchinson, 1958), 48.

24. Ibid.

25. Williams, *AmaZonia*.

26. Ibid.

27. Ibid.

28. Ibid.

29. Kevin Healey, "The Road Less Traveled," *South American Explorer* 24 (1990): 9, http://www.saexplorers.org/system/files/magazine/sae-mag-24.pdf.

30. Williams, *AmaZonia*.

Chapter 8: Spirit Love

1. Joe Fisher, *The Case for Reincarnation* (New York: Bantam, 1985).

2. Unless otherwise indicated, all direct quotations included in chapters 8 and 9 are taken from Joe Fisher, *Hungry Ghosts* (Toronto: McClelland & Stewart, 1991).

3. "Supernatural Investigator: Who Killed Joe Fisher? Part 2," *Supernatural Investigator*, 2014, http://www.visiontv.ca/videos/supernatural-investigator-103-who-killed -joe-fisher-part-1-the-trap-is-set/.

4. Ibid.

Chapter 9: Theater of the Gods

1. Michael Prescott, "The Dark Side of the Paranormal," *Michael Prescott*, 2014, http://michaelprescott.freeservers.com/the-dark-side-of-the-parano.html.

2. Vincent McCann, "A Christian Perspective on Ghosts and Hauntings," Spotlight Ministries, 2004, http://www.inplainsite.org/html/ghosts_and_hauntings.html#sthash .a2sxkQHV.dpuf.

3. Joe Fisher, *The Siren Call of Hungry Ghosts: A Riveting Investigation into Channeling and Spirit Guides* (New York: Paraview, 2001), 305.

4. Johanna Michaelsen, *The Beautiful Side of Evil* (Eugene Ore.: Harvest House, 1982).

5. Deuteronomy 18:10–12.

6. 2 Corinthians 11:14–15.

7. Revelation 21:8.

8. Fisher, *Siren Call*, 303.

9. "Supernatural Investigator."

10. Ibid.

11. Ibid.

12. Jonathan Zap, "The Siren Call of Hungry Ghosts," *Zap Oracle*, 2006, http://www.zaporacle.com/the-siren-call-of-hungry-ghosts/.

Chapter 10: The Mystery of Cicada 3301

1. Caitlin Dewey, "Absolutely everything you need to know to understand 4chan, the Internet's own bogeyman," *Washington Post*, September 25, 2014, http://www.washingtonpost.com/news/the-intersect/wp/2014/09/25/absolutely-everything-you-need-to-know-to-understand-4chan-the-internets-own-bogeyman/.

2. Chris Bell, "The internet mystery that has the world baffled," *Telegraph*, November 25, 2013, http://www.telegraph.co.uk/technology/internet/10468112/The-internet-mystery-that-has-the-world-baffled.html.

3. Michael Grothaus, "Meet the Man Who Solved the Mysterious Cicada 3301 Puzzle," *FastCoLabs*, http://www.fastcolabs.com/3025785/meet-the-man-who-solved-the-mysterious-cicada-3301-puzzle.

4. Bell, "The Internet Mystery."

5. "3301 ClevCode," *Bundlr*, 2012, http://bundlr.com/b/quarantine-interesting-stuff-that-should-be-kept-under-observation?order=inverse&view=timeline.

6. Jed Lipinski, "Chasing the Cicada: Exploring the Darkest Corridors of the Internet," *Mental Floss*, December 17, 2012, http://mentalfloss.com/article/31932/chasing-cicada-exploring-darkest-corridors-internet.

7. "The Internet's Cicada: A Mystery without an Answer," *NPR: All Things Considered*, January 05, 2014, http://www.npr.org/2014/01/05/259959632/the-internets-cicada-a-mystery-without-an-answer.

8. Chris Bell, "Cicada 3301 update: the baffling internet mystery is back," *Telegraph*, January 7, 2014, http://www.telegraph.co.uk/technology/internet/10555088/Cicada-3301-update-the-baffling-internet-mystery-is-back.html.

9. Ibid.

10. "CICADA 3301 Liber Primus Sacred Book," *Uncovering Cicada—Wikia*, 2013, http://uncovering-cicada.wikia.com/wiki/CICADA_3301_Liber_Primus_Sacred_BOOK.

11. "What Happened, Part 1," *Uncovering Cicada—Wikia*, 2013, http://uncovering-cicada.wikia.com/wiki/What_Happened_Part_1_(2013).

12. Tobias Churton, *Aleister Crowley, the Biography: Spiritual Revolutionary, Romantic Explorer, Occult Master and Spy* (London: Watkins, 2011), 44.

13. Richard Kaczynski, *Perdurabo: The Life of Aleister Crowley* (Berkeley, Calif.: North Atlantic Books, 2010), 18.

14. Ibid.

15. Ibid.

16. Aleister Crowley to Gerald Kelly, October 31, 1905, in Kaczynski, *Perdurabo*, 151.

17. Catherine Beyer, "Aleister Crowley, Thelemic Prophet," *Alt Religion*, 2014, http://altreligion.about.com/od/importanthistoricalpeople/p/crowley.htm.

18. Hugh B. Urban, *Magia Sexualis: Sex, Magic, and Liberation in Modern Western Esotericism* (Los Angeles: University of California Press, 2006), 118.

19. 2 Corinthians 4:4 NASB.
20. James Wasserman, *In the Center of the Fire: A Memoir of the Occult 1966–1989* (Lake Worth, Fla.: Ibis, 2012).
21. David Sheff, *The Playboy Interviews with John Lennon and Yoko Ono* (New York: Putnam, 1981), 61.
22. Erik G. Magro, "Revolution of the Mind: The Dreams of Aldous Huxley," *Conspiracy Archive*, 2014, http://www.conspiracyarchive.com/2014/01/30/revolution -of-the-mind-the-dreams-of-aldous-huxley/.
23. John W. Whitehead, "When the World Stopped to Listen," *Huffington Post*, May 29, 2012, http://www.huffingtonpost.com/john-w-whitehead/when-the-world -stopped-to_b_1552392.html.
24. David Sheff, "Playboy Interview: John Lennon and Yoko Ono," *Playboy Press*, January 1981, http://www.beatlesinterviews.org/dbjypb.int2.html.
25. Timothy Leary, *PBS Late Night America*, [undated interview], http://ac2012 .com/2012/08/05/aleister-crowley-myths-actually-true/.
26. "3301 Cicada Warning," *Pastebin*, January 4, 2013, http://pastebin.com/dHJ 6JNkr.
27. Ibid.
28. Ibid.
29. Ibid.
30. "Cicada 3301 Liber Primus Sacred Book."
31. "What Happened? Part 1."
32. Deuteronomy 32:39.

Chapter 11: The Zombie Apocalypse

1. "The removal of crania from burials, their ritual use and their disposal, generally in cranial caches, are the most particular characteristics of the funerary ritual in the transition to the Neolithic in the Near East." Jonathan Santana et al., "Crania with mutilated facial skeletons: A new ritual treatment in an early Pre-Pottery Neolithic B cranial cache at Tell Qarassa North (South Syria)," *American Journal of Physical Anthropology* 149 (October 2012): 205.
2. Bryan Nelson, "Stone Age people may have battled against a zombie apocalypse," *Mother Nature Network*, August 20, 2012, http://www.mnn.com/lifestyle /arts-culture/stories/stone-age-people-may-have-battled-against-a-zombie-apoca lypse#ixzz3H8D4KDQR.
3. Ibid.
4. "Zombie Killing," *Zombiepedia*, http://zombie.wikia.com/wiki/Zombie_Killing.
5. The trickster is often described in benign terms, which belies a more sinister nature. Dennis O'Neil, for example, in study materials for his Anthropology of Religion course at Palomar College, asserts: "Tricksters are frequently neither good nor bad." Yet far from the mischievous but harmless Wile E. Coyote image of the trickster, the examples O'Neil cites range from highly objectionable (theft of one's most valued possessions) to the genuinely horrific (stealing children). Dennis O'Neil, "Common Elements of Religion," *Anthropology of Religion: An Introduction to Folk Religion and Magic* (San Marcos, Calif.: Palomar College, December 11, 2011), http://anthro .palomar.edu/religion/rel_2.htm.
6. George P. Hansen, *The Trickster and the Paranormal* (Bloomington, Ind.: Xlibris, 2001), Kindle edition.

7. Quoted in C. W. Spinks, "The Laughter of Signs: Semiosis as Trickster" (San Antonio, Tex.: Trinity University), http://www.trinity.edu/cspinks/myth/trixsem.html.

8. George P. Hansen, "Demons, ETs, Bigfoot, and Elvis: A Fortean View of Ghosts," *Tricksterbook.com*, http://www.tricksterbook.com/ArticlesOnline/DemonsETs.htm.

9. Ray Hyman, *The Elusive Quarry* (Buffalo, N.Y.: Prometheus, 1989).

10. "The procedural errors in the Rhine experiments have been extremely damaging to his claims to have demonstrated the existence of ESP. Equally damaging has been the fact that the results have not replicated when the experiments have been conducted in other laboratories." Terence Hines, *Pseudoscience and the Paranormal* (Buffalo, N.Y.: Prometheus, 2003), 122.

11. John Zupansic, review of *Investigating the Paranormal* by Tony Cornell, *Ghost Village*, January 21, 2003, http://www.ghostvillage.com/library/2003/lib_cornell.shtml. See: Tony Cornell, *Investigating the Paranormal* (New York: Helix, 2002).

12. Michael D. Mumford, PhD, Andrew M. Rose, PhD, and David A. Goslin, PhD, "An Evaluation of Remote Viewing: Research and Applications," American Institutes for Research, September 29, 1995, http://www.lfr.org/lfr/csl/library/AirReport.pdf.

13. Sara Davidson, "Does Prayer Really Work?" *Sarah Davidson Blog*, 2014, http://www.saradavidson.com/does-prayer-really-work.

14. Po Bronson, "A Prayer Before Dying," *Wired*, December 2002, http://archive.wired.com/wired/archive/10.12/prayer.html?pg=4&topic=&topic_set=.

15. Ibid.

16. Ibid.

17. Jill Neimark, "The Power of Coincidence," *Psychology Today*, July 1, 2004, http://www.psychologytoday.com/articles/200407/the-power-coincidence.

18. There are suspicious cases, such as the circumstances surrounding the death of Joe Fisher.

19. Job 1:8.

20. Job 1:11–12, emphasis added.

21. Job 2:6, emphasis added.

22. Zap, "Siren Call."

23. Mark Macy, *Miracles in the Storm* (New York: Signet, 2001).

Chapter 12: The Restless Heart

1. Sharon Hill, "Psi, Sci (Sigh!) Sounds Sciencey," *Committee for Skeptical Inquiry*, June 11, 2014, http://www.csicop.org/specialarticles/show/psi_sci._sigh/.

2. William James, "Report on Mrs. Piper's Hodgson-Control," in *Proceedings of the American Society for Psychical Research* 3 (Boston: H. B. Turner, 1909): 586.

3. Hansen, *Trickster*.

4. Michael Harner, *The Way of the Shaman: A Guide to Power and Healing* (New York: Bantam, 1982).

5. This writer knows of no secular and atheistic ethnologists and anthropologists who object to such "ethnocentric" statements that "[assume] the superiority of the modern Western way of life," who have also jumped at the opportunity to reside permanently in a pre-literary society.

6. See: Stanley Jaki, *Science and Creation* (Lanham, Md.: University Press of America, 1990).

7. Harner, *Way of the Shaman*, 25.

8. Terence McKenna, *The Archaic Revival: Speculations on Psychedelic Mushrooms, the Amazon, Virtual Reality, UFOs, Evolution, Shamanism, the Rebirth of the Goddess, and the End of History* (New York: Harper, 1992).

9. "Ayahuasca Therapy with Graham Hancock," *Terra Forming Terra BlogSpot*, February 11, 2014, http://globalwarming-arclein.blogspot.com/2013/02/ayahuasca -therapy-with-graham-hancock.html.

10. Aleister Crowley, *Diary of a Drug Fiend* (Newburyport, Mass.: Weiser Books, 1977), 365.

11. Ibid.

12. Art Bell, "Graham Hancock: Supernaturals and Consciousness," *Coast to Coast*, December 28, 2006, https://www.youtube.com/watch?v=oxlrtNxEs0E.

13. Whitley Strieber, *Transformation: The Breakthrough* (New York: Avon, 1988), 181.

14. Karla Turner, "Abductions in the Gingerbread House," *KarlaTurner.org*, http ://www.karlaturner.org/articles/articles/turner/Abductions%20in%20the%20Ginger bread%20House.html.

15. Fisher, *Siren Call*, 252.

16. L. A. Marzulli, "An Interview with Joe Jordan: The Alien Interviews," *CE4 Research Group*, http://www.alienresistance.org/ce4marzulli.htm.

17. Ibid.

18. Ibid.

19. "Reptilian Vanquished, Disappeared in Name of Jesus Christ," *Alien Resistance*, February 13, 2013, http://www.alienresistance.org/91-reptilian-disappeared -in-name-of-jesus-christ/.

20. Ibid.

21. Ibid.

22. Romans 10:12–14.

23. Genesis 2:18.

24. Genesis 2:24.

25. Luke 11:33.

26. Revelation 12:12 NASB.

27. Runyan, *Magical Journey*, 35.

28. Augustine, *Confessions*, I.i.1.

29. Revelation 20:10.

30. Colossians 2:8–10.

INDEX

Abominable Snowman. *See* Bigfoot
Adamski, George, 49–50
 Flying Saucers Have Landed, 49
 influenced by "Madame" Blavatsky, 50–51
alien abduction, 66
 abductees transported to alien craft,
  66–67, 76–77
 intrusive medical "procedures," 68–69,
  76–78
 self-deception regarding, 69
 Stockholm Syndrome, 70
 thwarted by appealing to name of Jesus,
  185–188
atheism, 14
Atlantis, 16

Bigfoot, 16
 connections with demonic activity, 44–45
 lack of physical evidence for, 34–38
 phenomenon is unfathomable, 32
 reliable witnesses, 41, 44, 75
 trans-physical or interdimensional origin, 44–45
Bigfoot Field Researchers Organization
 (BFRO), 31–32
 Finding Bigfoot television program,
  37–38, 41
Bili ape, 32–33, 36–37
Blake, William, *The Marriage of Heaven
 and Hell*, 20
Blavatsky, "Madame" Helena Petrovna,
 17, 190

allegations of plagiarism, 105
 introduced the West to Eastern mysticism, mediumship, occultism, 17
 mastering psychic abilities in India,
  103–104
 rejected belief in Christian worldview in
  favor of "enlightenment," 104
 responsible for Percy Fawcett's ill-fated
  adventure in Amazonia, 100
 vision of lost civilizations, 100
Bryan, C. D. B., *Close Encounters of the
 Fourth Kind*, 75–82

Castaneda, Carlos, 16, 22ff, 182, 190
 controversy after death, 28–29
 don Genaro's "ally," estrangement from
  home and loved ones, 23–26
 initiation by don Juan Matus, 23
 Journey to Ixtlan, 24, 26
 secretive, cultlike inner circle of followers, self-described witches, 27
 Teachings of Don Juan, The, 23
Castaneda, Margaret, 25–26, 190
 final attempt to make contact with Castaneda, 27
 *My Magical Journey with Carlos Cas-
  taneda*, 26
Cicada 3301, 17–18, 145ff
 connection with Aleister Crowley,
  151–152
 cryptic puzzle leads to murky "darknet"
  depths of the Internet, 149

peculiar religious references, 150–151, 160–161

requires stunning level of sophistication and knowledge, 150

Crowley, Aleister, 18, 152ff, 190

impious maxim "Do what thy wilt," 155

Liber AL vel Legis dictated by "spirit guide," 152

rejected Christianity for a "radical compact with evil," 154

renaissance decades after his death, 156

secretive occult organization *Ordo Templi Orientis*, 155

Day the Earth Stood Still, The, 47–48

demonic entities, 15, 71

"deceiving spirits and things taught by demons," 15

present themselves interchangeably as positive or negative, 71

demonic virtual reality, 78–81, 180–181

devil, 14, 15

like a roaring lion, 14

murderer, liar, seeks to lead souls astray, 15

See also Satan

Doyle, Sir Arthur Conan, 88–90

Cottingley Fairies, charges of gullibility, 89–90

turns to Spiritualism after son's death, 88–89

Fawcett, Brian, 107–111

bizarre trans-dimensional relationship with "M," 108–109

concealed his father's spiritual quest, 109

Fawcett, Edward, 98–100

devotee of "Madame" Blavatsky, 98–99

Fawcett, Jack, 106

alleged reincarnation of an "advanced spirit," 106

Fawcett, Nina, 85–86, 112, 190

decline, 112

kept watch faithfully for missing husband and son, 112

Fawcett, Percy Harrison, 17, 83ff

expedition to lost city of "Z," 91–93

"Great Scheme" to develop mystic consciousness, 107

last reported sightings of, 112–114

lost city of "Z," 110–111

mediums directed planning and route of expedition, 106–107

obsession with Blavatsky, 106

reputation as the most intrepid and ruthless explorer, 88–89

search for missing Fawcett, 93ff

Fisher, Joe, 17, 116ff, 185, 190

fails to confirm Filipa's past life in Greece, 133–134

"guides" promote Eastern Mysticism, 125–126

"guides" reveal contempt for Jesus Christ, 124–125

supposed discarnate lover "Filipa," 120–123, 130–134

unable to collaborate past lives of guides, 127–129

unexplained circumstances of death, 141–144

writings steeped in Eastern mysticism and reincarnation, 117

Frankl, Viktor and Tilly, 12–13

God, 14

is love, 13

personal and infinite, 14

Gordon, Stan, 43

Han, Mrs., 42–43

Hancock, Graham, 182–184

Hastings, Robert, 63

UFOs and Nukes, 51–52

Henley, William Ernest, "Invictus," 16

Hopkins, Budd, *Intruders*, *Missing Time*, 65

Houdini, Harry, debunked psychics and mediums, 90–91

Huxley, Aldous, drug-induced hallucinogenic experiences, 19–21

Doors of Perception, The, 19–20

fascination with Vedantic Hinduism, pure consciousness, Brahman, 20

shared Aleister Crowley's vision for societal revolution, 157

Jesus, tempted by, rebukes devil, 14–15

cast out "unclean spirits" and demons, 140

deliverance in the name of, 186–188

exposes the malignant intent of the devil, 15

warns against those who love darkness rather than the Light, 61–62
Jordon, Joe, 185–188
Judeo-Christian worldview, 14

Keel, John, *The Mothman Prophecies, Operation Trojan Horse*, 60–61, 62
connection between aliens and occultism, 61

Lachman, Gary, *Turn Off Your Mind*, 21
Leary, Timothy, promoted hallucinogenic drugs, 21–22
admirer of Aleister Crowley, 158
Lewis, C. S., *The Screwtape Letters*, 70
love, God is, 13
evil entities exploit yearning for love and meaning, 184–185, 189–190
Huxley perceived "Love as the primary and fundamental cosmic fact," 21
universe suffused with love necessitates a Lover, 21
unquenchable yearning for, 13

Mack, John, 59
alien abductions "transcendent" rather than physical in nature, 80
Macy, Mark, *Miracles in the Storm*, 173
similarities between spirit world "Marduk" and Riverworld novels, 175–176
Matus, don Juan, 16, 23
McKenna, Terence, 182

Paranormal Conspiracy, subverts search for ultimate meaning, 13
baffling mingling of suggestive evidence and misinformation, 81
cosmology without God at the center, 16
engages in spiritual terrorism, 71
spreads chaos and fear, 71
subverts rational order of the universe, 16
thwarted by "the name that is above every name," 18
trickster phenomenon connected to, 165
paranormal phenomena, 16–17
baffling assortment of mysterious cryptids, 44
connections between various manifestations of, 165
Society for Psychical Research, 166

paranormal worldview, belief in world controlled by unseen forces, 14
shaman plays vital role in appeasing angry and vengeful spirits, 14
Patterson, Roger, "a cheat, a liar, and a thief," 40
Patterson-Gimlin Bigfoot film, 34, 38–40
Paul, apostle, speaks of "rulers of the powers of the air," 17, 191
"the god of this world has blinded the minds of the unbelieving," 156
warns that "Satan himself masquerades as an angel of light," 140
Plato's cave, 20
Powell, Thom, 30–31

reincarnation, central tenet of paranormal conspiracy, 16
deceiving spirit guides teach, 124
endless reincarnations needed to satisfy one's karma, 104

Sagan, Carl, 59–60
Sasquatch. *See* Bigfoot
Satan, rebuked by Jesus, 15
binding of, 170–174
seeks to attack the good and entice souls to their damnation, 180, 189
Schaeffer, Francis, 14
Serpent, in the Garden, 16
disturbing hallucinogenic visions of huge serpents, 182
instigated rebellion against the Creator, 181
Shamanism, disruption of the divine order leading to chaos and decay, 179
pays homage to the reptilian enemy of God, 182
Silva, John and Hilda, 9–12, 190
spirits, 15
deceiving mortals, 15
exploit yearning for love and meaning, 184–185, 189–90
powers constrained, 171–172
Stargate Project, 167–168
Strieber, Whitley, 17, 64ff
alleged abduction by aliens, 66–70
attributes dark, sinister motive to the aliens, 71
Communion, Transformation, 69

demons from evil realm of darkness, 69, 185
"loving" aliens and self-deception, 69–70
wife Anne's illness, 72–74

Targ, Elisabeth, 168–170
transmigration of souls. *See* reincarnation
trickster, 18
can temporarily assume material forms, 164
characterized by disruption, unrestrained sexuality, disorder, 164
dual stratagem of fear and deception, 178
enigmatic forces making fleeting appearances, 164
Turner, Karla, 62–63, 184

Unidentified Flying Objects (UFOs), 16, 17,
bewildering diversity of alien types, 58
Fermi Paradox, 53–56
from another dimension, 62

intention to transform human society, 63
majority of incidents occur late at night, 61–62
nuclear weapons a mere cosmic pinprick, 56–58
observable universe, 53
Washington, D.C., sightings, 47–49

Vallée, Jacques, 61

Yeti. *See* Bigfoot
"You will be like God," 16
Cicada 3301 allusion to, 161
New Age belief, 45–46
seductive assurance of the Serpent in the Garden, 16

"Z," lost city of, outpost of extraterrestrial gods, 100
zombie apocalypse, 14, 162ff
decapitated skeletons at Tel Qarassa in Syria, 162–163

Timothy J. Dailey has degrees from Moody Bible Institute (B.A. Bible, Theology), Wheaton College Graduate School (M.A. Theological Studies) and Marquette University (Ph.D. Religion and Ethics). He has also studied at Jerusalem University College and Hebrew University, Jerusalem.

Dr. Dailey has lived and taught on three continents. He met his Swiss wife, Rebekka, in Bethlehem, where their first two children were born. Dr. Dailey taught courses on theology and on the historical and archaeological background of the Bible at Bethlehem Bible College, the Jerusalem Center for Biblical Studies and Biblical Resources Study Center. While living in Bethlehem during the Gulf War, Dr. Dailey wrote *The Gathering Storm* (Chosen, 1992)—the first of a dozen published books as well as numerous articles.

Since returning to the States, Dr. Dailey taught theology at Toccoa Falls College before becoming senior editor for Chuck Colson's nationally syndicated "BreakPoint" radio program. Dr. Dailey has also served as senior fellow for policy at the Family Research Council in Washington, D.C. He and Rebekka have five grown children and live in Northern Virginia.